"Graham is a highly effective present[] and gets straight to the point. His book [] as he is in person."
Nick Jeffery, CE[] [] Global Enterprise

"I don't know anyone who could wear the label "the presentation coach" more confidently than Graham."
Daniel Finkelstein, Executive Editor, *The Times*

"I use Graham's system strictly and religiously in every speech. In fact on almost every important occasion when I need to get a message across… You will never regret buying and using this book."
George Clarke, MD, Heidelberg UK

"Graham helped me develop my very own presentation style, true to myself, with high impact and focused very much on the audience"
Phil Clarke, CEO Designate, Tesco

"Graham's approach is ruthlessly robust and utterly practical. This book is the next best thing to seeing him in person, and much less of a strain on your budget."
Matthew Wilson, CEO Brit Global Markets

"The quest for authenticity is now at the heart of the leadership challenge, but why do so many of us find it impossible to be ourselves when presenting? Davies's compelling book illuminates all the pitfalls and provides a simple guide to allowing personality into presentations - radical stuff indeed!"
Andy Street, MD, John Lewis

"Whether you are a Prime Minister, chief executive or anyone else who needs make an impact, then you must read this challenging and innovative book by Graham Davies.
Neil Sherlock, Partner, Public Affairs, KPMG

"This book really annoys me, because I wish Graham had written it 20 years ago. Then maybe I wouldn't have had to spend countless hours being tortured by Investment Bankers who think that "presenting" means reading out all the words on all their slides."
Richard Klein, MD, Bank of America Merrill Lynch

"Never again will you commit the crime of Death by Bullet-Point."
Penny Philpot, Group Vice President,
Worldwide Partner Services, Oracle

"Graham Davies is a talented gagmeister who shows that the best way of exposing a bad argument is with a good joke. "
Boris Johnson, Mayor of London

"Graham completely reframed my approach to presenting. His approach works!"
Otto Thoresen, CEO, Aegon UK

"A process that you can use no matter what the situation. I heartily recommend it."

Michael Gove MP

"Graham forces you to be absolutely clear on the message you're trying to get across. He gives you the confidence to feel that it's you the audience wants to see and hear all the time; rather than them being happy to sneak an occasional glimpse through the undergrowth of your slides."

Mark Angela, CEO, Pizza Express

"Reading his book will spur you on to win your own presentational race."

Richard Dunwoody, twice winner of the Grand National

"This book is not a coaching guide for the faint-hearted. Prepare to be beaten into being bloody brilliant!"

Francis Edmonds, broadcaster, author and professional speaker

"In this book Graham shows you a preparation process and the delivery techniques that will give you a professional edge whether you are a speaking veteran or a complete beginner".

Kaye Adams, broadcaster

"Graham's coaching has not just massively helped me in every presentational arena, it has had a profoundly positive effect at every level of the Conservative Party, ranging from parliamentary candidates to Cabinet Ministers and even the Leadership itself."

Mark Field MP

"I have been speaking professionally for years but since being coached by Graham, my performance has reached a new level. If you have to present or speak to groups and the impact you have matters at all, you had better buy this book!"

Shaun Smith, author and professional speaker

"This book is precisely like its author: sometimes crassly confrontational, but always wittily informative."

Andrew Roberts, broadcaster and author

"*The Presentation Coach* really packs a punch…. You are left fully focused, fighting fit and forever equipped to out-perform the competition."

Joanna Hall, TV fitness guru and author

"Rugby and presenting are both strenuous activities carried out in front of a critical audience. I will never ask Graham's advice about Rugby, but I will always rely on his advice about presenting."

Rob Andrew

"If you are serious about the way you present yourself or your business, you simply have to read it.

Saira Khan, broadcaster, author and runner-up in *The Apprentice*

THE PRESENTATION COACH

Bare Knuckle Brilliance For Every Presenter

Graham Davies

CAPSTONE
be inspired!

Library of Congress Cataloguing-in-Publication Data

9780857080448

A catalogue record for this book is available from the British Library.

Set in 11.5 on 12.5pt Adobe Caslon Pro-Regular by Aptara
Printed in TJ International Ltd, Padstow, Cornwall

CONTENTS

Why yet another book about Presenting?   *vii*

1   The Essentials   1
2   Know your Audience   15
3   Make the Statement   33
4   Hard-Core Content   51
5   Write it, Read it, Edit.   67
6   From Famous First Words …   83
7   Nail it all Down   97
8   Show it … if you really must   115
9   Control Yourself   135
10 Control the Day   151
11 Control Q & A   167
12 Raise a Smile   177
13 Adapt to After Dinner   193
14 Should I Accept the Invitation   211
15 Challenging Business Situations   219
16 Challenging Personal Situations   243

Pipeline Summary   263
Key Bare Knuckle Terminology   264
About Graham Davies   266
Acknowledgements   267

Index   268

WHY YET ANOTHER BOOK ABOUT PRESENTING?

For the last 20 years, I have combined the roles of professional speaker and presentation consultant, coaching people on how to get their spoken message heard, assimilated and acted upon.

I made my first speech when I was 13. I was not particularly worried about the prospect of appearing in front of an audience because I had already been performing in various English speaking competitions from the age of 10. However, these competitions involved learning poetry, extracts from the Bible or scenes from plays. I did not have to create any of my own words. Suddenly having to be the originator of what was coming out of my mouth was rather scary.

I did not have a fear of speaking. But I did have a fear of *preparing* to speak.

That childhood experience convinced me of the need for a preparation process that could be relied upon to generate material that worked. I don't want you to have that sinking feeling in the pit of your stomach as you sit in front of a blank piece of paper or empty computer screen thinking, "I just don't know where to start."

Later, at university, as an audience member at the Cambridge Union Society, I listened to some superb speeches from a wide variety of outstanding speakers, ranging from Enoch Powell to Barry Humphries. Even though I knew that I was often listening to brilliance, it was not unusual to find it hard to remember what they had said the next day – or even a few minutes after they had finished speaking. Many other audience members told me that they had a similar problem.

So, as a way of enhancing my own listening experience, I tried to summarize and crystallize the very best of what guest speakers were saying ... while I was listening to them. That way I could remember and pass on their "greatest hits" in conversation with others. At last, I could actually define what was so good about a given speech.

I soon realized that encapsulation of a speech's best material in a pithy, concise statement also worked as a *preparation* device as well as a listening device. I gradually worked the concept into the speeches I began to write for myself and other people.

Soon after I left Cambridge, I was speaking 2 or 3 times a week and advising many other people on their speaking activities. I was also doing speeches literally every day in court, working as a barrister. However, I churned out what I had to say without really knowing the most efficient and effective way of doing so.

In 1994, I met Dan Bond and we co-founded the presentation consultancy Straight Talking. His presentational background was in theatre stage management and conference production ... somewhat different to the direction from which I entered the game.

We had both already done several years of presentation coaching, but we knew that our advice merely polished the surface of presentations rather than going to the core of them. Therefore, we carried out a great deal of research into the presentation techniques that were prevalent at the time.

We were simultaneously encouraged and disappointed by the fact that we couldn't really find any author whose advice we really rated. The exception was the first section of a book by Sandy Linver called *Speak and Get Results* (1991). She advocated a deep understanding of the audience as an essential part of speeding them to accept the presenter's 'message'. This really made sense to us, because it was already a core attitude in our own coaching.

She gave this point of audience acceptance a name: 'Point X'. We prefer the way that we use the somewhat less exotic term, the 'Result'. But her allusion to a 'map' and the audience's 'journey' also struck a chord with our own experience.

However, her concept of the 'message' was just not precise and robust enough. We felt that there needed to be a more concrete concept at the very core of presentation preparation. We also did not like her approach to the opening words of a presentation, which encourages you to avoid controversial statements and instead tell them something they already know. When it came to presentation delivery, we were uncomfortable with her emphasis on breathing and voice exercises, as we knew that very few clients ever had the time or inclination to actually do them in the real world.

But how could we ensure that the audience never sets one foot off the crucial path towards enlightenment? None of the vast array of manuals in the market provided a truly comprehensive, yet simple, *linear process* for presentation *preparation*. Everything that I had experienced at Cambridge and in my own speaking and coaching career up to that point had taught me that creating content had to be approached in a vastly more systematic way.

In this book I show you the rigorous method that Dan and I have created and developed over 15 years. It can help *anyone* prepare and deliver a presentation. Our distinctive approach includes the use of a **Preparation Pipeline** that forces you to approach presentation creation in a straight line. It helps you to create a finely honed, memorable and repeatable Micro-Statement to control the writing of material. We show you how to use special filters to turn draft material into final content. We advocate the injection of sharp, 'sit-up-and listen' attention-grabbing phrases throughout presentations, from beginning to end.

All this is combined with a skeptically minimalist attitude to PowerPoint (carefully tempered by additional practical suggestions from top-class international professional speaker and Slideware athlete Warren Evans) and carefully calculated advice on the power and horror of humour.

We have honed our Preparation Pipeline through time spent coaching dozens of different companies and hundreds of individuals. Our clients have included IBM, Ford, Bain, KPMG, Deutsche Bank, Tesco and Vodafone ... as well as politicians, celebrities and Olympic athletes.

The result is a process that we now call the **Bare Knuckle Method**. It works for a lot of people in a lot of situations, and it can certainly work for you.

Chapter 1

THE ESSENTIALS

You present more often than you think. It does not have to involve you standing up in front of a seated audience ... although in business that is the scenario that causes the most anxiety for most people for most of the time. In fact, in the workplace and beyond, you present every time that you attempt to change someone's viewpoint by using spoken words.

Presenting is an every day activity for everyone. Those that do it well are likely to get to the top of their chosen profession. It is such an important activity that it should not be left to chance. In the 2010 UK General Election, it was the unexpectedly brilliant presentation performance by Nick Clegg in the televised debates that propelled the Liberal Democrats from Oblivion to Government, as well as securing for himself the second most powerful job in the country. The techniques contained in this book can make excellent personal communication a certainty instead of a lottery, whether you are a Prime Minister, product director, preacher or primary school teacher.

This book deals with the wide variety of presentational scenarios. For some people, these situations may occur regularly. For others the invitation to speak may come

1

unexpectedly and demand a huge amount of thought and care in preparation: for instance when asked to give a eulogy. However, I suspect that you are reading this book because you want to improve your performance in the 'you-in-front-of-more-than-five-people-in-the-audience' sort of situation. Accordingly, the first six chapters focus on this scenario, which I will from now on call the *Formal* Presentation. Once you've mastered this scenario, you can master any of the other situations that I cover in later chapters.

To help you achieve this success, the **Bare Knuckle Method** uses a **Preparation Pipeline** that you can walk through with the maximum of speed and the minimum of angst.

This step-by-step methodology is tried-and-tested and will allow you to get results you will be proud of every time you present. You may not always get a Knockout, but you can always win on points, facing every speaking challenge in the knowledge that Bare Knuckle techniques give you the best possible chance of success.

Why Bare Knuckle?

I use the term because you need to fight constantly for the privilege of your audience's attention. You are not fighting *against* the people in front of you….but you are fighting against all the other facts, figures and opinions in their minds at any given moment. For a few minutes, it is your information and attitude that must gain the ascendancy.

The Bare Knuckle Fighter uses a vast range of unconventional combat techniques to get the results he needs, without being bound by a restrictive set of rules. In the same way, the Bare Knuckle Presenter is not confined by the stiff Marquess of Queensbury style of Death by Bullet Point.

This is why the central aspects of my coaching have always embodied a rather *driven* attitude. This idiosyncratically assertive approach involves asking you to go through a Preparation Pipeline every time you need to speak.

The key characteristic of the Pipeline is that it forces discipline on you without stifling your creativity.

The methodology may not be a total guarantee (I have to leave some of the responsibility with you!), but it will definitely take the pain out of the process and make you a real contender.

The Challenge

You may well dread giving presentations. But always bear in mind that audiences dread *listening* to them even more. They fear that their time is going to be wasted. They worry that they are going to hear material that they have heard many times before. More than anything else, they worry that they are going to be bored.

So, why bother with a presentation? Why not just send the information by e-mail?

The difference must come from you, the presenter: *you* must provide the reason why.

In a century where executives frequently receive more than 100 e-mails a day, information on a screen can never be totally compelling. A presentation is real communication, with life and breath and flesh and blood. It is the human element that makes the difference. Only a live presenter can provide information with inspiration and impact. The words are merely ammunition ... you must be the weapon.

But there are too many presentations. Most of them are too long, whereas the human attention span has never been so short. **I strongly believe that very few presentations should ever be longer than 20 minutes, no matter how brilliant the presenter.** In fact, some of the most popular business presentations in the world are given at TED conferences (see www.TED.com). They have assembled dozens of the world leading thinkers in virtually every discipline to share their ideas, inventions and interpretations. The main reason that the presentations are so compelling is that they strictly enforce a time limit of **18** minutes.

Knowledge and intellect are useless without the power to communicate. There are certainly more communication tools available than ever before, ranging from PowerPoint to the marker pen. However, the best tool remains *you*. The main problem you face now is a lack of time: time to prepare and time to deliver.

A presentation is not about building a lifetime relationship. You should treat it like an *affair* that is short but memorable. It should have some great highlights, but be over quickly.

The prayer of the 21st Century audience is:

'Let me hear something new that makes listening worth the effort. Please don't let him make me yawn.'

The mantra of the 21st Century presenter should be:

'Say it. Support it. Shut it.'

This book shows you how.

The Method

I can summarize the Bare Knuckle content preparation methodology very quickly. It is based on the conviction that every piece of spoken communication should have a **Micro-Statement** at its core. A Micro-Statement is what you would say to a given audience if you only had 10 seconds in which to say it. It is the shining jewel that you hope will dazzle and persuade them to think and do what you want them to do.

This is the five-step **Preparation Pipeline** I mentioned earlier that you must hard-wire into your psyche:

1. Know your audience (through thorough analysis)

2. Decide where you want to take them (by getting to understand what they really need to hear)

3. Create a Micro-Statement (which will propel your audience along your chosen path)

4. Support the Micro-Statement (to provide the evidence for the case you are arguing)

5. Spike your beginning and your ending (so that the words with which you started and finished will still be going through their head long after you left the room)

At the start of the next six chapters, you will find a sequence of headings which makes up the detailed sections of the Pipeline, so that you always have a clear idea of exactly where you are in the process.

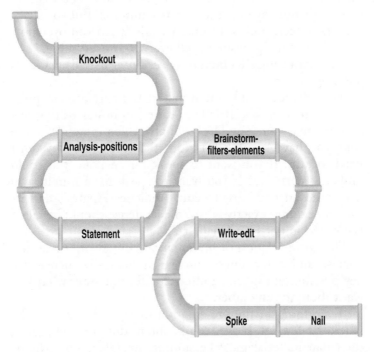

I am sure that you are looking forward to finding out what a Knockout Result is, but I am going to leave that until the next chapter. You are probably less excited at the prospect of Audience Analysis, because it does sound as if it might be rather ... *anal.* But it does not have to involve a spreadsheet or a tedious computer programme. For the largest conference audiences, you may have rather too much information potentially available from the organizer about every single individual. You cannot hope to cater exhaustively for every audience member.

But when you are talking to three people around a table, personal information is much more desirable for you.

Even audiences at weddings and funerals can be effectively analyzed, so that your speech contains the most compelling material from the life of the groom or the deceased.

Remember that, for the audience, the prevailing atmosphere is one of sickly dread, not just dislike. You need to constantly fight against this negative mindset. But you strike the first effective blow in this struggle when you overcome the overwhelming desire to tell everybody everything.

A presentation that includes *everything* usually achieves *nothing*.

An audience is only interested in the part of your presentation that makes their lives easier, so brutal editing is a fundamental courtesy. They will always be grateful for the time you have spent cutting out the stuff that they don't need to hear. If you want to speak for an hour, you could probably start now. If you want to speak for a minute you may need an hour just to edit. Audience Analysis and its role in deciding exactly where the audience should be taken is covered in detail in Chapter 2.

The encapsulation of presentation content in a relevant, concise and compelling sentence dramatically increases a key possibility: **that the audience will remember what you want them to remember.**

Everything in the presentation must relate back to the Micro-Statement. If a piece of content does not support it, then that material must be summarily culled. The Micro-Statement is both the transport and the guidance mechanism that will take the audience to where you need them to go. It is also the highly valuable gift that you want your audience to take away with them. How to create this legacy will be dealt with in detail in Chapter 3.

Although the Micro-Statement is crucial, it rarely thrives on its own ... hence the need to support it.

Just because you have said a particular thing does not mean that the audience will remember it. A presentation should not be a sequence of lists for memorization, like a conveyor belt of prizes in a game show: if they remember three key points that support the message from a 20 minute presentation, then you have done very well indeed. If you are absolutely determined to include 17 key points, then you have a problem: the audience may have stopped listening before you have stopped talking. It is your duty to edit for *impact*. You will find guidance on structure and editing in Chapters 4 and 5.

Many times I have heard a client utter this heartfelt cry:

'I'm alright once I get going, but I just don't know how to start.'

Imagine that a presentation is like your steamiest love affair. The moment when it began should be unforgettable. I am sure that you didn't waste any time with pleasantries like

'It really is a great pleasure to meet someone as attractive as you, and I look forward to the opportunity of getting to know you better, but before we start, let me show you this organizational chart so that you can see where I fit into the Davies family....'

Or maybe you did and you still find the Internet a more forgiving place to conduct romance. Nobody has time for fluffy pleasantries.

How to Spike the beginning and end of your brief encounter with the audience is passionately described in Chapter 6.

The Preparation Pipeline described in the first seven chapters is the paramount source of comfort that you will find in this book. I urge you to get into the habit of using it to decide on what to say in every speaking situation. It is vital that you absorb the concepts in the Preparation Pipeline so at the end of Chapters 2 to 5, you will find a list of Action Steps which summarize how to use the Pipeline to create your Core Content.

When you learned how to drive, the sequence of steps in a hill start probably seemed awkward at first. But now it is a manoeuvre that you can do almost sub-consciously. In the same way, the first few occasions that you walk through the pipeline, it may feel a bit awkward ... but the way will become smoother and more lubricated each time, so that it eventually becomes an automatic thought sequence whenever it needs to be.

Chapters 8 to 10 deal with both the high-tech and low tech tools that can be used to back up the gorgeous content you have forged. Very few 'normal' people have the inclination or ability to be actors. Attempting to learn content as if it were the script of a play is as unrealistic as it is frightening. But it is still necessary to keep your words on track somehow. Chapter 7 discusses the merits and methods surrounding notes, paper scripts and teleprompters.

Chapter 8 asks you to make a seismic shift in thinking. I want you to accept this piece of corporate heresy:

'It is possible – and often highly desirable – to make a compelling formal business presentation without using PowerPoint.'

I have made this statement many times in the boardrooms of Fortune 500 companies. It is often greeted with the same angry stare that the Vatican must have given to the first chap who told them that the world is round.

The idea that a presentation should be carefully and powerfully phrased right from the outset goes against most mainstream practice. Traditionally (i.e. over the last five years), when an executive is asked to make a presentation, his first reaction is to reach for his laptop and turn up the PowerPoint to warp factor 10. The 'presentation' becomes a numbered sequence of slides, which form a corporate collage of bullets, numbers and charts. He feels no need to prepare what he is actually going to *say* because he thinks that he will be magically guided by what is on the screen. He can 'talk to the slides' like a digital Dr Doolittle.

The purpose of Chapter 8 is to give you a supremely practical methodology and show you how to adapt it to get the result you need ... even when you *are* using PowerPoint.

Chapters 9 and 10 are based on the viewpoint that your delivery skills must be as sharp as your editing. There is no point in spending millions of dollars on the development of state-of-the-art skis if they are only going to be worn by Eddie the Eagle. I totally disagree with the view expressed by Jerry Weissman in *Presenting to Win* (2003):

'When the story is right, the delivery itself tends to fall into place, almost magically so.'

This is a very dangerous attitude, which runs the risk of wasting all the hard work put into getting the content right. Many times we have seen excellent content delivered very badly indeed, thus losing most of its value. Preparation and delivery should not be seen as different disciplines. They are as inextricably linked as Turnover and Profit ... or Plague and Pestilence.

Chapter 9 is about controlling your nerves and honing your delivery skills. Nerves can be a good thing: a natural survival response that sharpens the senses. But for some people they are a horrible barrier to effective performance. Every presenter should seek to control nerves rather than eradicate them. They can be ruthlessly channelled so that they force you to prepare properly and concentrate on the real needs of the audience. Negative anxiety can become positive anticipation

This chapter also shows you how to maximize control over your body and your voice in a way that accelerates you into the presentational fast lane. I will encourage you to have a Bare Knuckle attitude to delivery, which means always getting to the point as directly as possible.

Chapters 10 and 11 show you how to adapt your delivery skills to the demands of the day itself. It is also about controlling the environment in which that delivery is going to take place. This involves knowing what to look for, what to ask for, and what to insist on. And I show how to make the relationship between presenter, audience, projector, screen and microphone as effective as possible.

A monster that lurks in the minds of many presenters is the thought of having to answer questions in front of an audience. Bleak horror is only justified when you don't possess the right combination of strategic attitude and tactical practicality that awaits you in Chapter 11, without once mentioning bankruptcy proceedings in the USA.

A smiling audience is a receptive audience. However, the creation of laughter is an exact science that requires the use of precise formulae. When used incorrectly, humour can have disastrous effects. Chapter 12 lets you skip through this anti-personnel minefield.

Chapter 13 is about the high wire act of the presentation circus. An After Dinner Speech can be the most deliciously entertaining way to end a meal. It can also be the most appalling torture. Heavily interwoven with stories about my own post-prandial triumphs and disasters, this chapter identifies how to make the experience enjoyable for everyone in the room.

Whether you have been asked, volunteered or required to speak, you must be sure that it is the most appropriate thing to do. Chapter 14 contains the criteria by which you should make the decision. Not speaking at all may be the correct choice if you have identified a more effective alternative.

The Restrictions

The Spoken Word has dominated my working life, but I am acutely aware of its limitations. A presentation may enlighten, persuade and entertain, but it can never cover the whole topic. A presentation with exhaustive detail becomes a lecture to an exhausted audience. A lecture is designed to cater for the needs of a studious group of people. Even the smallest detail might make the difference between passing and failing an exam, so the academic audience does its best to write down nearly every word that the lecturer says.

However, I guarantee that no audience member in the entire history of public speaking has *ever* made a verbatim note of what has been said in a business presentation.

What's the difference between a Bare Knuckle Presenter and a lecturer?

About 300 grand a year.

Technology both encourages and caters for the microscopic 21st Century attention span. If you are watching television, you know that you can instantly go to another channel if you get bored. Even if you are watching a DVD, your finger will be quivering over the Fast Forward button if the story gets bogged down. When you are surfing the net, if a site takes more than 10 seconds to download, you will probably go elsewhere. Corporate audiences are similarly impatient.

Bare Knuckle presenters must seek to find an exquisite blend of brevity, clarity and impact...or else their presentations will become victims of the 21st Century One-Click-And-I'm-Out-Of-Here mindset.

My own fundamental mindset is that:

A presentation is any spoken communication designed to change someone's point of view.

The key word is 'change'. All effective presentations include an element of challenge to the status quo ante. A presentation should never consist of a sequence of words that merely act as a reminder of what the audience already knows: reminders are never compelling. The definition above uses the word 'someone' instead of 'audience', because many common presentational scenarios involve speaking to just one person (e.g. phone calls).

For a presentation to be a worthwhile experience for both presenter and audience, there must be an overwhelming reason for those words to be said. If you just want to remind someone, don't make a presentation. Send an e-mail instead.

In this book, the words 'speech' and 'presentation' are synonymous, although we accept that the two words are sometimes used to describe widely differing scenarios.

David Cameron addressing the Conservative Party conference would be giving a speech. A finance director introducing his cost-cutting initiatives to the chief executive would be giving a presentation.

In fact, these two situations are at opposite ends of the same communication continuum. There are many techniques that are equally vital for both scenarios. You must decide which techniques are needed for your audience at that time

You will never see Cameron using PowerPoint (hallelujah). Your finance director's presentation will never be preceded by a warm-up from William Hague (again hallelujah).

But the word 'Presentation' does have a particular implication for many listeners: for them, the word implies that the speaker is going to provide something for the audience to *look* at. I accept that this is corporate reality, despite my earlier assault on PowerPoint. But whatever is shown, it must be used sparingly and created with care if it is to have any impact.

Here are some typical requests for presentations in a business context:

'I'd like you to get the team fired up to beat their target.'

'Can you bring us up to speed on your project?'

'Tell us some more about your company.'

'Can you present our product to an interested prospect?'

'Please give us the findings of your research.'

There are countless other scenarios that involve presentation, including:

- complaining about service;
- answering questions under pressure;
- being part of a panel discussion;
- media interviews;
- team pitches;

- delivering a eulogy;
- introducing another speaker;
- telephone conferences;
- wedding speeches.

All of these should still involve selective use of the Bare Knuckle method, and are dealt with in Chapters 15 and 16.

The Result

Every single presentation situation involves the transfer of information. Audiences can vary in size from 1 to 1000. Environments vary from boardrooms to ballrooms. But the same fundamental principle still applies: a presentation should be designed to change an audience's point of view and, ideally, *get them to take an action as a result of this change.*

If information is being presented, the audience must be told what to do with it.

It would be much easier just to 'brain-dump' the information, with this being the prevailing mind-set:

'I've told them absolutely everything. It may have taken nearly three hours ... but I've done my job.'

Information on its own is rarely enough. If any change is to take place there must be ideas, enthusiasm and attitude.

To position these components appropriately, you must take into account how your audience feels, and seek to reposition their feelings relative to the material they are hearing. Hanging information on an emotional hook will significantly improve retention: the audience will remember the way that you made them feel long after they have forgotten the facts you have given them.

Unlike the vast majority of presentation books, this one will show you a precise, adaptable, audience-focused preparation process, as well as how to deliver the material created by that process. It is a process that can be used even when the time available is extremely limited. Presentations are not like Ancient Rome: they *can* be built in a day. Or an hour. Or even five minutes … if the time is used with discipline.

I will show you how important it is to choose the right words long before you say them to the audience. Fantastic slides will *not* make your presentation stand out. Fantastic words *will* because so few presenters bother to think carefully about their words before they actually present them. You will discover that your vocal chords can work unaccompanied by the clicking of a mouse.

Incidentally, I also dislike the idea of telling a 'story'. This is what Arthur Andersen, Enron and Lehman Brothers used to do. It is what Bill Clinton was so good at. The word has an unintentional whiff of embellishment and inaccuracy. I hope that none of your audiences think that you are merely telling them a story.

There is no fictional story-telling in this book. I only give you what you need. And not a word more. No waffle, no chitchat, no platitudes.

There are many presentational habits that are so prevalent that they have become accepted orthodoxy. Sadly, these same habits are actually encouraged by many of the other books on the subject. Throw those books away now. OK, not all of them. I will refer to the tiny minority that include credible techniques. But I will not hesitate to attack outmoded, clichéd nonsense. If you wanted a book that is humbly deferential to its competitors, then you have wasted your money.

This jack-booted approach is absolutely necessary:

'Few new truths have ever won their way against the resistance of established ideas save by being overstated.'

Isaiah Berlin

Many presentation coaches will hate this book. A few will fall in love with it. I hope you do too.

CHAPTER 2

KNOW YOUR AUDIENCE

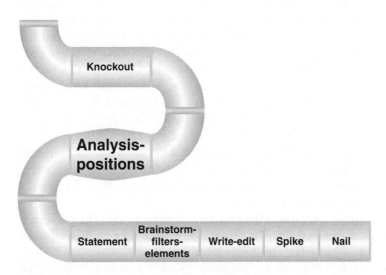

A more comprehensive title for this chapter could be 'Know your Audience ... *and where you are going to take them*'. This is because all presentations are about leadership. An effective presentation leads the audience from where they began, to where you would really like them to be. You should not be trying to have a pleasant chat: you must be compelling, vigorous and firmly focused on where your words will take them.

Remember, the opportunity to present is an enormous privilege. The audience has invested their most irreplaceable asset: *their time*. They have also consented to you being the only person in the room who is talking. They will quickly withdraw that consent if they feel that their time is being wasted. This means you must, at all times, fight to keep their attention, while ensuring that your time in front of them is as potent as possible.

You are definitely *not* looking for the lowest common denominator. This is a phrase that suggests you will come up with shoddy, off-the-shelf remarks. What you need to find is the *Highest* Common Denominators. These are the cleverest and most sophisticated factors you can possibly rely on while continuing to win over the majority of the audience. This is the sort of information that allows you to make your eventual words a high-quality, classily bespoke product.

To get the best result, you must be very selfish about the result that you want to achieve. But the most effective selfishness is that which is combined with sensitivity: sensitivity to the needs of the audience. You cannot be audience *driven*: this implies too much loss of control. But you must use your control to become audience *focused*.

My experience with dozens of FTSE 100 companies over the last 15 years has taught me that there is a desperate need for *more* audience focus. Only rarely is there an overlap between what the presenter wants to say and what the audience needs to hear.

It is only when the audience is certain that the presenter has focused on what they need, that they will be able to focus on what the *presenter* needs.

To give you some insight into what a presenter should be sensitive to, here is a list of 10 things you will *never* hear an audience member say:

'That presentation should have been much longer.'

'His message was far too easy to understand.'

'I needed to see 10 more slides.'

'Why can't they get more words on each slide?'

'Oh how I ache for more numbers and statistics!'

'I think they should have packed a few more presentations into the conference.'

'He seemed too well prepared.'

'His enthusiasm really put me off.'

'My time is not really important.'

'He made the subject too enjoyable.'

It's enough to make anyone feel deflated. So, when you are sitting in front of a blank computer screen, feeling daunted by the task ahead, where can you find the necessary presentational stimulus?

There is no one single source of speaking strength, but a fundamental ingredient is a grasp of where the presentational route begins and ends.

This may sound very straightforward; surely no one would go to all the effort of making a presentation, without being certain of what they wanted to get out of it? Sadly, the answer to that question is: *oh yes they would!*

The Bare Essentials

Before you do anything else, ask yourself a simple question:

'Why am I making this a presentation?'

The answer *should* be:

'Because I need to create a result that is best achieved by communicating face-to-face.'

When you have established that presenting is the right thing to do, the second, and even more important, question is:

'What am I trying to achieve?'

Every presentation must be created to achieve something specific. You must define precisely what this is very early on in the preparation process. If you don't know where you are going at the start, then your audience won't know where *they* should be at the end.

Most presentation books tell you that there are many types of presentation. In fact there is only one type. Every presentation must be a *persuasive* presentation. Both the delivery and the content of the presentation must be equally persuasive, because ...

Well-delivered crap is still crap.

A Knockout?

The first stride in the creation of persuasive *content* involves defining with exacting precision what it is that you would like to achieve. Let's return to my core contention that you have to continually fight for the audience's attention. In any form of combat, the ideal result is total and immediate victory, with your opponent lying on the ground with no resistance left in them. You need to decide what would constitute such a comprehensive conquest in a presentational sense. In other words, what Knockout Result are you aiming for?

A **Knockout Result** is what, in an utterly ideal world, you would like to accomplish with your target audience.

I strongly suggest that you make a stab at deciding your ideal Knockout Result by just using your gut instinct. Don't let your presentational ambition be strangled by too much cold reality.... at this stage.

Here is a range of varied business goals that you might seek:

- I want to persuade them to absorb all of this important data and then act on it.
- I want to persuade them to invest their entire Pension Fund with us.
- I want to persuade them to adopt every aspect of my cost-reduction plan.

- I want to persuade them to double my bonus.
- I want to persuade them all to feel motivated.

The requirement for persuasion does not stop at business presentations. There is the same requirement in many other contexts:

- I want to persuade them to remember the deceased fondly with tears and laughter.
- I want to persuade them all to vote for me.
- I want to persuade them to give money to my charity.
- I want to persuade them to focus exclusively on this aspect of the New Testament.
- I want to persuade them all to laugh.

After Dinner Speeches are probably the only presentations where it is possible that the *only* Knockout Result you want is audience laughter. The success or failure of this type of speech is gauged almost entirely by the amount and intensity of the laughs stimulated. In all other presentations, laughter may be something that merely *helps* you to achieve the desired outcome. Sometimes it will get in the way. The power and danger of humour will be covered in Chapter 12.

Analyze your audience

Relatively few boxing matches are decided by a Knockout. Most bouts go the full distance, with one fighter winning on points. Although the winner would have loved to triumph with one punch, a 15-round victory is still a very satisfactory winning achievement.

With a cynical eye, look again at the possible presentation goals listed earlier. You will see that some of those ideal results are just not going to happen, no matter how persuasive you are. Your gut instinct-based stab at what the Knockout Result should be now needs to be tempered by audience analysis.

The audience will be much easier to persuade if you have precise knowledge of the position they will be in mentally and metaphorically when they first encounter your spoken words. Only when you have gathered sufficient information about the audience will you be able to answer the question:

Is the Knockout Result you have selected feasible for this audience at this time?

If you are asking for commitment to a particular course of action, you must know whether anyone with the right level of authority is present in the audience. You must know whether they are already committed to similar projects that would swallow up resources that your project would need. You must know whether the logistics are possible now or in six months: your presentation might be too early (or too late). After proper consideration, you may realize that the answer to the question is painful: the desired outcome is just not reachable. In that case, you will have to do something that may feel even more painful: you will have to accept that you will not be able to get your ideal Knockout Result.

If it is clear to the audience from the outset that the result you seek is simply not viable, you may end the presentation *further away* from what you want. Your long-term credibility may also be damaged. If you fail, you fail very publicly.

When I am playing golf, I know that I will never be able to use the driver to blast the ball over a water hazard 250 yards from the tee. Instead, I would take a five iron and deliberately hit the ball well short of the hazard. My desired outcome becomes realistic. The credibility of my 28 handicap is enhanced.

In the same way, your ideal Knockout Result may be:

'I want them to agree to my three-phase consulting project'

After you have found out as much as you can about your audience, you may have to scale back your desire and aim for something less spectacular:

'I want them to implement the first phase of my project immediately and consider the next two phases within three months'

If you aim at a credible winning achievement, you won't lose your balls in the lake.

The Preparation Pipeline

Presentational situations vary enormously, which means that you may vary the degree of rigour with which you use the process ... sometimes using every single stage in full, sometimes only individual concepts. But you should *always* use at least some of it.

There may be internal events at which you *have* to present, times when a third party *asks* you to present and occasions when you *want* to present. Whether you are the one who has decided to speak or the job has been thrust upon you, there is no excuse for lack of planning or analysis – that is unless you are happy to risk failure. I have witnessed a lamentable lack of preparation on many painful occasions. Those weak presentations may have been informative or even entertaining, but they still left me with the feeling that the presenter wasn't really sure where they wanted to go.

Using the Preparation Pipeline to follow the process covered by this and the next five chapters minimizes the risk of you losing your way, or your audience when you present. The Pipeline encourages you to come up with a simple, linear (and thus easy to follow) result, at the same time as allowing some complex and creative thought as you progress.

Defining Positions

To be an effective presenter and leader, you do have to be rigorous in your planning of the mental route along which you will lead the audience. To do this you need to first establish exactly where you currently stand, as if placing a 'you are here' arrow on a public information map. This is the first point in the Pipeline. To do this, you must identify your audience's thoughts and feelings about your presentational topic. This will enable you to define what I call the audience's Starting Position.

The **Starting Position** is what the audience thinks, knows or feels about your presentational topic before you start your presentation.

It is perhaps more accurate to say that the Starting Position is your very best calculated guess about what the audience initially thinks, knows or feels. There will inevitably be an element of subjectivity involved in making this calculation.

After you have worked out the Starting Position, you will then, and only then, be able to work out precisely what you want to say to all those people who are staring so intently at you. On the vast majority of occasions, a total Knockout Result will be out of reach. However, a perfectly desirable (if less formidable) winning achievement is still within your grasp. I call this desired and practically attainable audience mental state the Finishing Position.

The **Finishing Position** is what you want the audience to think, know or feel at the end of the presentation, having taken into account the full practical reality of the situation.

You can only decide on what the Finishing Position should be after you have gathered sufficient intelligence about the people to whom you will present.

Gathering Presentational Intelligence

You should treat this as an essential part of the process. There are no short cuts. You have to glean knowledge from yourself, the organizers and your audience. After all, the only truly effective leader is one who understands himself *and* the people that he is trying to lead. You need to know all about yourself and about the people to whom you will present. The main source of information about this latter group is the very people who have asked you to present.

Know yourself

Ask yourself the hardest question of all.

'Why am I doing this presentation?'

For many people, the answer is often:

'Because I have been told I have to.'

Presentations are often dropped in the lap of an unsuspecting executive after an arduous round of corporate pass-the-parcel. If the time-bomb lands on you, make sure that you are using the right communication medium, in the right way, with the right people at the right time.

Written documents and e-mails, used in isolation, are rarely as persuasive as live presentations. However, even presentations to small numbers of people are expensive to stage. Look round the table at the next presentation you attend and calculate the total hourly value of those present in the room, not forgetting the time it took for them to get there. Bear this figure in mind as you consider how long your presentation should be.

What about video-conferencing? Getting your point across on screen is much harder than when your audience is in front of you in the same room. Video presentation and live, face-to-face presentation are two very different skills. Ideas and information are best bought and sold between individuals in the same room. Video-conferencing should be seen as a last resort.

Questions for the people who ask you to present

When speaking at a conference or to an audience outside your organization, here are the 10 basic factual questions to ask the client contact/host/organizer:

1. How many people will attend?

2. What is the age range?

3. What is the gender split?

4. What nationalities/ethnic groups will be present?

5. What are the levels of education / qualifications?

6. What is the spread of job titles of those present?

7. What organizations are represented?

8. Who will speak before you?

9. Who will speak after you?

10. Who will introduce you?

When dealing with an internal audience or a client that you know well, most of the core audience information (from questions 1 to 7) will be readily available. But beware of complacency. Because the presenter already knows the basic information about the audience he may wrongly believe that he knows *everything*.

Questions 8, 9 and 10 are relevant for *all* speaking situations.

After getting the basic facts, your next step is to get inside the heads of the audience. As Stephen Covey would say, 'Seek first to understand and then to be understood'.

Earlier on in this chapter, we reviewed what the typical audience *never* thinks about issues such as time, delivery and content.

However, I can assure you that every audience member *is* thinking a combination of the following...

- *'Please tell me something I don't already know.'*
- *'Please don't waste my time.'*
- *'Please give me something that makes my life easier.'*

Few people will relish being condemned to PowerPoint Purgatory. Remember that an audience is an inherently selfish entity.

You must treat them as you would a professional dinner party bore who is unhappy unless you are talking about *him*. This is the universal core audience attitude:

'I've had enough of thinking about my needs. What do YOU think about my needs?'

The success of your presentation depends on how much what you want to say coincides with what they want and need to hear.

Successful presenting is a process of constantly answering the questions that the audience has on their minds. But even though you must be audience focused, you must not allow yourself to be audience *dominated*. After all, you do have your own agenda. You want to answer their urgent questions *and* achieve what you want. To do this, you have to map out the journey you want to take the audience on, with a clear beginning and an even clearer end.

Not everyone feels that this should be done in advance of the presentation. Bizarrely, some books recommend that you save a large chunk of your research until you *begin* the presentation! They suggest that you start by asking the audience questions, and build their answers into your presentation as you go along.

I vehemently disagree with this approach. It is far too late to start your research at the moment you begin delivering the presentation. The audience will immediately feel that you just couldn't be bothered to prepare properly: they just weren't important enough.

Interaction is no substitute for properly prepared content.

After all, if it is not worth preparing in advance, it is not worth the audience making the effort to listen. Preparation-on-the-hoof is disastrously discourteous.

You should not allow yourself to be audience *dominated*, but a certain amount of audience *obsession* is entirely healthy.

It is possible to prepare too much.

It is possible to rehearse too much.

It is *never* possible to know too much about your audience.

Questions for the people that you are presenting to

All the questions below are designed to help give the answer to this vital, overall question:

'What must I give them so that I get what I want out of the presentation?'

Or putting it in a more emotive way:

'Where is the fire that my presentation can put out (or stoke up)?'

The questions touch on feelings as well as facts:

- What interests you about this subject?
- What was the reaction to the subject from previous presentations?
- What do you already know about the subject of the presentation?
- What do you *have to* know about this subject?
- Do you feel negative, positive or neutral about coming to this presentation?

You should ask these questions even if you are speaking to an internal audience (i.e. from your own company). Just because you see them every day, it does not mean that you will automatically know their attitude towards an important forthcoming presentation.

Any communication is only as good as your understanding of the people with whom you are trying to communicate. Call them, go and see them or, as a last resort, e-mail them. They will feel surprised and flattered by the effort you are clearly making to tailor your words for them. Bespoke always feels better than off-the-peg.

With larger audiences, you may have to go out of your way to get the phone numbers and e-mail addresses of a significant proportion of your audience. I'm not asking for the impossible here: if there are going to be 500 people in the audience, a 'significant' proportion means 10 people; if there are going to be five people in the audience, you should try to contact them all.

When you make contact, ask the five key questions identified above. The answers will allow you to produce content that is compelling, because of its relevance to that particular audience. Do try to get information from an actual conversation rather than asking them to merely fill out a form online. The information you get will have more life and value than anything you get from someone who is merely tapping on a keyboard.

Nevertheless, if you are preparing a keynote for a large audience, you may still feel that you would like to make at least some brief cyber-contact with as many of your audience as possible. It is possible that the organizer of the event will agree to act as an information conduit from the audience to you. He may agree to send to each possible audience member a brief survey. I recommend www.survey-monkey.com as a source of relevant templates.

All of the previous questions are important, but not as important as the next one. If you only have the chance to ask an audience member one question, it should be this:

'What can I tell you in my presentation that you need and don't already know?'

Only the most obnoxious corporate egotist will refuse to answer that question. After all, it is in his best interests to make sure that his time is not being wasted.

We realize that many important people (or people that think they are important) are often very difficult to speak to by phone or e-mail. But you will probably be able to get through to a PA. The best PAs are not defensive about the likes and dislikes of their boss. If a Chief Executive has an aversion to 45-minute presentations with 50 slides, then they will tell you. I hope. Even the most protective PAs may give you five minutes of phone access to their boss once you make it clear that this could save half an hour of his time during the presentation itself.

Knowing that you have done your very best to discover the needs of the audience will give you an enormous psychological boost when you finally come to deliver the presentation. You can be confident that you will not fail because of ignorance ... maybe because of arrogance, stupidity and lack of rehearsal ... but not ignorance.

There is a subsidiary benefit that you get from all the effort you put into getting to know your audience: it boosts your standing in they eyes of the audience well before your presentation starts. Every person you speak to will probably tell at least two other future audience members about the conversation you have had. You will quickly gain a reputation as someone who cares about their needs ... and if a good proportion of the audience feel that you already care about what they want, they will be that much more sympathetic to what you want ... even before you have started to present to them.

On some occasions, it may feel as though your Audience Analysis has been almost too successful. You have found out that many member of the audience have widely differing concerns. It can then be very difficult to decide on a Starting Position that is an accurate reflection of their amalgamated viewpoints. In these circumstances, you have to look for the **Highest Common Denominators**. These are the most distinctive and sophisticated items that a majority of the audience agrees are the most important.

I have deliberately used the word 'majority' because it is unlikely that there will be many issues about which everyone will agree completely. As a result, no presentation can please all of the people all of the time. There are very few countries where major set-piece speeches are met with such universal approval that it is unwise to be the first person to sit down at the end of a Kalashnikov-inspired standing ovation.

Clarifying your Positions

Your newfound knowledge will be a springboard into the writing process. The information from your audience analysis gives you your Starting Position: where the audience is at the beginning of your presentation. This embraces what they know, think and feel about your subject *before* you've had a chance to influence them. This must include their gut feeling as well as their factual knowledge.

You should be able to put the Starting Position into words, for instance:

'Before the start of my presentation, the audience will already know about the background of me and my company. They are certainly interested in my product, but they do not know about the results we have achieved with our recent clients.'

Make yourself go through the discipline of actually writing out the Starting Position. This will force you to clarify exactly where they stand.

During the presentation, your aim will be to lead the audience from the Starting Position to the Finishing Position. The Finishing Position is the mental state you want them to have the end of the presentation, having considered all the circumstances. Again, you should be able to define the Finishing Position in a sentence:

> 'At the end of my presentation, I want the audience to be so impressed with our software that they would like to see whether it is compatible with their current software.'

The Finishing Position should be a precise thought. You must know exactly where you want the audience to go before you try to take them there. You never want the audience to be thinking, 'This is quite interesting, but I don't really know where he is going with this'.

Once you have decided what your Finishing Position might be, then test it with the following questions:

- Are you sure that the required mental leap between the Starting Position and the Finishing Position is not too great?

- Are you sure that the audience is in a position to be able to take the action you are proposing?

- Are you sure that this is the right occasion to present this information?

- Are you sure that you are not asking them to absorb too much information in the time available? Remember that the mind cannot accept what the bottom cannot endure.

I am aware that the sheer number of questions that I suggest you ask may put you off the whole process of Audience Analysis. I also realize that you will often just not have the time to go through them all. The **Action Steps** below therefore include just the questions that you absolutely *must* know the answer to. They encapsulate all the issues that might arise if you asked all the other questions that are spread throughout the chapter. Use them as your quick-and-dirty analysis when you don't have time to be slow-and-clean.

If you use the approach in this chapter, you will already have gone a long way towards breaking the shackles imposed by the blank computer screen in front of you, thus making it likely that you will have the vigorous impact you need.

If the audience has moved from the Starting Position to your desired Finishing Position by the time you have finished talking, then the presentation has been a success.

The next chapter tells you about the mechanism you can use to get them to do precisely that.

Action Steps

1. Ask yourself what you want to persuade your audience to do.

2. Decide what Knockout Result you are aiming for.

3. Research your audience, using the following questions as a bare minimum:

   - **Who are they?** Identify the individuals and categories of individuals present.
   - **Why are they together in that room?** Make sure that you know whether they are primarily there to hear you or for another reason entirely.
   - **What do they want to hear?** They may have not worked this out, but if they have, you should have made an effort to find out what it is.
   - **What do they need to hear?** This might be entirely different to what they want. The onus is on you, the Presenter, to work this out for them.

- **What must you tell them during the course of the presentation that gives you the best chance of you getting what YOU want from having given the presentation?** Of course, this is the Holy Grail. No-one can get this right every time they present, but it is something that you should strive for every single time.

4. Using the answers to the above questions, write out your best estimate of the audience's Starting Position.

5. Decide whether your ideal Knockout Result needs to be scaled back to a more attainable Finishing Position.

CHAPTER 3

MAKE THE STATEMENT

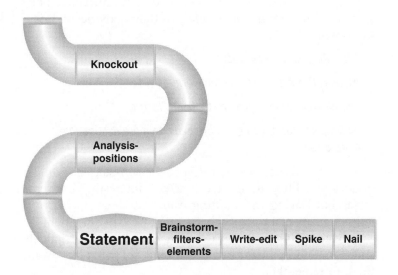

This chapter is about the device that pushes the audience to where you want to take them. The device should also be a lot more than that: it should also contain the words that you want them to remember and cherish long after you have left the building. This is why it cannot merely be a 'message'.

'Messaging' is not a potent presentational weapon, because it is too vague and ill-defined a concept. To be effective, anything that is intended to encapsulate the most important words in a presentation must be carefully defined and precisely targeted. Only then can it be an effective way of getting your audiences to absorb, appreciate and act on what you say to them.

Audiences Today

We are bombarded by far more information than we were 10 or even 5 years ago. But our capacity to absorb it has not increased at the same time. We try to filter out what we really need, but the filtration process is hard work. Advertising agencies actually take advantage of this limitation. They work hard to capture the essence of their activities in a few sharp words:

'CNN: Real News, Real Fast.'

'Federal Express gives you the world on time.'

'For all your creature comforts, Cook Electric.'

'In BA Club World, you get more beds, to more destinations, more often.'

These words act as a snapshot of the company or product in question. They are merely a taster – interesting in themselves, but leaving you wanting *more*.

Each is an example of what I call a Macro-Statement.

A **Macro-Statement** is a sequence of words that quickly and compellingly captures the essence of what you want them to remember.

A Macro-Statement should be short, snappy and memorable. But you don't need a Saatchi and Saatchi sized budget to create one. I saw this on the shop-front of a small delicatessen in Manchester:

'Churchill's Sandwiches – making lunch your Finest Hour.'

All these examples share a characteristic that is at the same time their greatest strength and their greatest weakness: *they are created to be seen by the whole world rather than by a specific group of people.*

Macro-Statements are usually designed to be read, rather than said. They are not tailored in any way. They are designed to capture the attention of as many people as possible, but only for a few moments. They are not designed to make people think carefully about that particular organization or product. The effect is meant to be superficial. They are meant to be a floodlight rather than a spotlight.

Macro-Statements have been used a great deal in the world of British political presentation. In 1979, the Conservative Party based their General Election campaign around the following Saatchi and Saatchi inspired Macro-Statement:

'Labour isn't working.'

A photograph of a dole queue stretching out into the distance cleverly reinforced the verbal Macro-Statement. This was a very successful exercise in superficial mass persuasion.

For the 2010 General Election, the Tories used two different Macro-Statements:

Vote for a Change

And

We're all in this together

These two statements did not possess the elegant pithiness of the 1979 Macro-Statement. I am certain that their inherent vague weakness was one of the major factors in the Conservatives not securing an overall majority.

However, the encapsulation of a *live, spoken presentation* must go a lot further than this. It must stimulate the audience to consider a subject in much more depth. The only way of doing this is to hone the encapsulation specifically for each audience.

It then becomes something that I call a Micro-Statement.

Creating a Micro-Statement

A **Micro-Statement** is a sequence of words that quickly and compellingly captures the essence of your presentation in a way that is specifically shaped for the needs of a specific audience at a particular time.

The Micro-Statement is essential to the success of the whole presentation. It is the catalyst in the carefully orchestrated process of moving the audience from their Starting Position to the Bare Knuckle Presenter's desired Finishing Position.

The two concepts of the Finishing Position and the Micro-Statement are closely related: one is meant to drive the audience to the other. The easiest way of grasping their relationship is to think of them as being connected by the word because:

The audience will be persuaded to adopt the point of view in your desired Finishing Position *because* of the information and concepts contained in the Micro-Statement.

The Micro-Statement is the distilled essence, the hard core diamond at the heart of the presentation. It is what you would say if you only had 10 seconds in which to say it. It is what you want the audience to remember *above all else*. In fact, if the audience remembers nothing else apart from your Micro-Statement, you will have achieved far more than the vast majority of presenters.

A sharply defined Micro-Statement is what really stops a presentation from being a dim, diffuse light source and turns it into a penetrating laser beam.

A clear Micro-Statement is particularly vital when ideas are being cascaded down an organization. You don't want those ideas to be diluted. The creation of a short, relevant and memorable Micro-Statement avoids this. The benefits should be implicit in the Micro-Statement. Consider the result you want if I were to take a member of your audience to one side and ask them 'Can you quickly tell me the most important thing that the presenter was trying to get across?' The answer you want that audience member to be able to give is the exact words of the Micro-Statement.

A Micro-Statement has six essential characteristics. It should:

1. Be created specifically for only one audience.

2. Feel crucial to that audience.

3. Stimulate audience thought.

4. Be one sentence long.

5. Be simple enough to be memorable.

6. Contain in itself its own justification.

It is quite a challenge to get all these characteristics into one sentence. That is why creating the Micro-Statement is the most time-consuming part of content preparation. The time spent is well worth it: if you don't have a clear and memorable Micro-Statement, you will not make a clear and memorable presentation.

Creating Material from a Micro-Statement

Let's say that you are a sales executive for a company that manufactures golf equipment. You have two different audiences to address. The first audience is a group of Golf Shop owners who of course want to make money from selling on equipment to their customers. The second audience is a group of actual golfers who are the end-users of the equipment out on the course. Both presentations have a similar Starting Position and desired Finishing Position.

Starting Position: before the start of the presentation, the audience knows very little about the product other than vaguely positive rumours, but are keen to know more.

Finishing Position: the audience will feel that *Lazerforce* is the range of clubs that satisfies their needs.

But each group will have different concerns. This means that we need to create a different Micro-Statement for each audience.

Micro-Statement to Golf Shop Owners...

'Lazerforce golf clubs are the clubs for you because their high profile in the press makes them extremely easy to sell with a high margin.'

Micro-Statement to Golfers...

'Lazerforce golf clubs are the clubs for you because they hit the ball the longest possible distance, in a straight line, for the least amount of money.'

These Micro-Statements are less snappy than the corporate Macro-Statements I have listed above. This is an inevitable consequence of precise targeting. Tailoring and glitziness rarely go together.

But both Micro-Statements satisfy the six criteria. Both have been specially created to help with the needs of a specific audience.

Different issues arise from each Micro-Statement. The first Micro-Statement, for the golf shop managers, is positioned to match the sort of concerns they might have:

'Public profile'

- What adverts is the manufacturer running?
- What are their plans for radio and TV?
- Are they putting on any special events?
- Which professionals are they using to endorse the product?
- Can selling this product be profitable for me?

'Easy to sell'

- How many were sold last year?
- How many from shops like mine?
- What discounts do I get?
- What special offers will be available?

The second Micro-Statement, for actual golfers, addresses issues that are relevant to anyone who actually plays the game:

'Longest possible distance'

- How far?
- Further than my current club?
- Can someone of my standard use it effectively?
- Who says that it is so good?
- How does it to manage to do this?

'In a straight line'

- What sort of tests have they done?
- Does that really apply even to someone as crap as me?
- Can I see a demonstration

'Most competitive price'

- How much?
- How does the price compare to the competition?
- Is it really worth it?

The presentations should contain the answers to these questions. Thus the Micro-Statement is the focal point for the preparation process. Everything must come from the Micro-Statement.

You should use the Micro-Statement to force discipline on yourself. It must become the foundation on which your presentation is built.

As you build up your content, you will consider many pieces of material that you may or may not end up in your finished presentation. These may include statistics, facts, quotations, anecdotes, jokes and many other things. Everything in the presentation should relate back to the Micro-Statement. As each piece of possible content occurs to you, think:

'Does this help to convince the audience of the value of my Micro-Statement?'

If it doesn't, then leave it out. More detail will be given in the next chapter about how the Micro-Statement should be used to drive the writing process.

Here is a Micro-Statement that Dan Bond (my partner in Straight Talking) created for the chief executive of a multi-national telecoms provider when he was speaking to his Pan-European staff:

'To expand in Europe, we must convince our customers that we can respond to their needs 24 hours a day.'

He used 'convince' rather than 'assure' because it was clear to him and his senior team that a significant campaign of persuasion was needed. It is possible to create a Micro-Statement that endorses a product as well as showing some vision. In the following example, a marketing director of an international insurance company ensured that his in-house audience was aware of the deeper implications of doing their job well:

'We have a duty to encourage consumers to buy Protection Products and discourage them from simply ignoring the issue.'

One of our clients is the president of his country's Fund Management Association. In his speech at the Association's annual dinner, he needed a Micro-Statement that not only captured the urgency of the situation in his industry, but which was also simple enough for the attendees to remember (after a bottle of wine) and convey to their colleagues the next day.

This is what he said:

'Despite the unpopular reforms, if we are going to increase our market share, we must help the government to carry out a major international marketing campaign.'

This Micro-Statement was blunt without being offensive to any of the politicians present.

Mind you, if you want offensive, I can do that as well. Micro-Statement in a courtroom should not be subtle ... after all, they have to be understood by judges and juries. I have successfully used this:

'My client could not have committed this crime because he clearly has all the intellect of a kebab'

The creation of an effective Micro-Statement should be agony. It should be about as easy as passing a melon. Your first attempt will rarely turn out to be the one you use in the finished presentation. Every word of the Micro-Statement must be worried over, because this is the shining legacy that you will leave behind for your audience. Treat it like the precious jewel you want it to become.

I realize that I could be accused of glorifying preparational masochism. Well, I can offer some comfort: when you finally hit upon the right Micro-Statement, *you will know immediately*. It is like love at first sight. Most prospective house-buyers know they have found the right place the moment they cross the threshold. The right Micro-Statement will have the same effect on you.

The mental process required for arriving at a Micro-Statement varies for each individual. Some people I know are so concise and confident in the way that live their lives that the use of Micro-Statement merely crystallises the way they already communicate. At the other end of the spectrum there are those who are innately so verbose that their attempts at a Micro-Statement seem to have been edited by Tolstoy.

Whatever your initial mindset, it is usually best to try going through a combination of structured questions combined with good-old-fashioned, gut-instinct, plucking-something out of the air. The process involves asking yourself, and maybe also trusted colleagues, a sequence of **Micro-Statement Creation Questions:**

1. What is it that is most striking about the information that I want to convey?

2. Is there anything that appeals to both the heads and the guts of this audience?

3. Is it something new to them?

4. If they absorbed and believed this, would it drive them over the Because Bridge towards the desired Finishing Position?

5. Can you put it into one sentence?

6. Would you be very disappointed if they did not absorb, accept and act on this?

7. Are you sure that it will be enough to make them want to pass it on to other people?

There is another, more hard-nosed analogy that may help you to grasp the concept of the Micro-Statement: think of yourself as a fighter pilot and the Micro-Statement as a guided missile. You identify the target (Audience Analysis/ Starting Position). Next, you decide precisely what effect you want the attack you have (Finishing Position). Then you select the right weapon (create the Micro-Statement). But you can't launch the weapon until it has 'locked on' to the target. You have to feel that the Micro-Statement has locked on so securely that it will hit your audience precisely at that point where their guts and their brains intersect.

Now that we are in the mood for combat, we should mention that politicians should use Micro-Statements more often. In November 2002 Iain Duncan Smith (then the leader of the British Conservative Party) spoke at the Institute of Directors Annual Dinner at the Grosvenor House.

He needed to mount a brutal attack on the Chancellor's record that would strike a chord with the business-focused audience in front of him. The following Micro-Statement was the weapons platform that we created for him:

'If Gordon Brown continues to clog the arteries of the country with the cholesterol of tax and borrowing, then we are heading for an Economic Coronary.'

Although I have yet to influence any of Barack Obama's speeches, he does seem to use his own version of Micro-Statements. His victory speech in November 2008 brought to life what has perhaps become the most over-quoted political slogan of this millennium so far: the somewhat grating Yes We Can.

I deliberately use the word 'slogan' and not 'Micro-Statement' because of its simplistic nature. Arguably, it was in fact a *Macro*-Statement, because it was designed to appeal to the whole country rather than just the million or so people standing in front of him. It was a phrase that Obama tried to get the audience to chant back to him…an endeavour in which he was only partially successful. Call-and-response of this type is unlikely to catch fire anywhere beyond an evangelistic church.

The other problem, apart from its simplicity, has been the ease with which it can be parodied … hence Republican comedians asking the question:

Can he come up with an affordable Health Care Plan? *No, he can't.*

More disturbingly, the phrase was hijacked by a character in the sitcom *Glee*, who started a campaign for the return of school corporal punishment with the phrase Yes We Cane.

On the other hand, Obama took a completely different approach to his inauguration speech. It was a much more restrained and statesmanlike piece, in keeping with the occasion and the problems that his country faced. The phrase that most closely approximated to a Micro-Statement was:

'It's time to get up off the ground, dust ourselves down and get on with the job of getting our country back on its feet.'

No-one will be chanting this in 10 years' time. It does not have the simple (perhaps simplistic) accessibility of Yes We Can. Again, because the worldwide audience was so huge, it was arguably a *Macro*-Statement. But it certainly was an effective encapsulation of what he wanted his audience to remember and act upon at that particular moment. It therefore succeeded as a *Micro*-Statement. And crucially, the majority of media commentators picked it up as the phrase that epitomized his maturing attitude to the massive task ahead.

Testing the Statement

You don't have to rely on your gut instinct. You can test whether you have got the right Micro-Statement by seeing whether it satisfies the following **Micro-Statement Testing Questions,** some of which deliberately repeat concepts brought up in the Creation questions:

- Can the Micro-Statement be easily remembered?
- Does it deal with the burning issue?
- Is it bold enough to capture the audience?
- Will the audience see it as something so precious that they will want to tell other people about it?
- If the audience remembered and acted on the Micro-Statement, would that be a good enough result for you?

Each question needs a resounding 'YES'. It is only when you have the right Micro-Statement, that you have the chance of creating a compelling presentation.

Time limits

When I first introduce the concept of the Micro-Statement to a client, they usually wrestle with it and eventually grow to embrace it once they have put it into practice a few times. But they often challenge me in these terms:

> 'Most of my presentations have to be longer than 30 minutes, because of the sheer amount of information that I have to get through. Surely one Micro-Statement can't run through that amount of material?'

I am always pleased when I am confronted with this, because it means that the client has put a lot of effort into working out how the concept really works. It also means that they have worked out its limitations.

There can be no precise mathematical formula, but I firmly believe that a single Micro-Statement cannot sustain more than 20 minutes of live presentation. If you know that you will definitely be longer than that, *you should consider whether there should be more than one sub-presentation, with more than one Micro-Statement*. This will help to make the overall presentation more manageable for you and more memorable for the audience.

This splitting process may be straightforward or a real challenge, depending on the subject being covered. A presentation that happens to be about three different geographical areas may well be split into three sub-presentations, with different Micro-Statements relating to each area:

- The Northern division is struggling so badly that we may have to replace the whole management team.
- The Midlands division is surviving reasonably well in a tough market, so they should be encouraged to sustain their efforts.
- The Southern division is doing so well that we should see if any of their techniques can be copied by the other divisions in the long term.

A presentation that describes your organisation's current practice before going on to recommend how that practice should change could nicely divide into two. The Micro-Statement of the first presentation might be:

'The Barnsley factory uses a superb process that has been the envy of the bread-making industry for 100 years.'

The Micro-Statement for the second presentation focuses on the future instead of the past:

'The only way to increase our production levels and maintain quality is to split the process between three different factories.'

An hour-long political speech may lend itself to several Micro-Statements. David Cameron is currently not a user of the Bare Knuckle methodology, but concepts similar to Micro-Statements are sprinkled throughout his speeches. The keynote speech he gave to the 2009 Conservative Party Conference was more memorable for its tone than its content. But there was one striking Cameron-style Micro-Statement that lit up a central chunk of the speech:

'The Conservative Party is the only party that can effectively fight poverty in this country.'

It stimulated an immediate standing ovation and was the main focus of media reports that day and the next. Look back at the Micro-Statement testing questions and see how well Cameron satisfied my criteria. The legacy was certainly strikingly memorable, confronted a vital issue and stimulated tough questions (how can we afford to do this?).

He certainly wanted the audience to be excited by a radically fresh Tory Agenda, so it probably drove the audience a significant distance towards the Finishing Position that he desired.

But when we get to the last Testing Question ("if the audience just remembered and acted on this, would this be a good enough result?"), we can see that the Micro-Statement is only partly successful. There were many other issues in the speech that Cameron also wanted the audience to embrace and act on. Nevertheless, this particular Micro-Statement worked extremely well, as long as it is seen as the

Micro-Statement for just that particular sub-section of the speech.

Section Differentiation

Of course, you do not have to go through the agonies of Audience Analysis before creating the Micro-Statement for each sub-section of a long presentation: The audience will remain a constant factor. But the Finishing Position of each section will have to be calculated, for instance:

At the end of Sub-Presentation 1, I want the audience to agree that we need to recruit more staff in the Bristol Office.

At the end of Sub-Presentation 2, I want the audience to feel that the sales team in the Birmingham office have done an outstanding job and should be given an extra bonus.

And so on. Two separate Micro-Statements are needed to drive the audience to those different Finishing Positions.

Adaptability of the Concept

Micro-Statements work in a wide variety of situations.

When I was preparing the eulogy for my mother's funeral, my desired Finishing Position was for the audience to remember her with tears and smiles. I included the following Micro-Statement very close to the start:

'I am certain of this: she would want us to remember her as a proud Scot, but more than that, as a proud and loving mother.'

It was also these words that gave me the discipline to get through the writing process in the midst of the inevitable emotional turmoil. They helped me to focus on the stories.

I knew of her early life in Glasgow as well those from when she became a wife, parent, friend and my number one fan.

The vast majority of this book focuses on face-to-face communication, but Micro-Statements can be used in phone calls. For instance, in a situation where you are phoning to complain about poor service, it can set out the agenda of the call and give a strong indication of what you would like to achieve.

I once had a very bad experience with the travel service associated with a leading credit card company. I had spoken to one of their consultants and asked her to find me a hotel next to the Dead Sea. An exchange of e-mails followed over the next two days. She suggested one in Eilat and I had to point out that this was next to the *Red* Sea. Her next suggestion was a Turkish Hotel, which I had to remind her was by the *Black* Sea. The longer our correspondence continued, the more obvious it was that she did not even have the most basic grasp of geography.

So I gave up. But I certainly wasn't going to leave it there. I eventually got through to a senior manager, and after the initial pleasantries, I said the following Micro-Statement:

'Because of the high annual fee I pay you, I expect a much higher standard of service than I have received over the last 48 hours....so let's see what we can do to compensate me.'

The manager thus knew exactly what the situation was and what I wanted to get. Five minutes later, I was offered, and graciously accepted, a £200 reduction of my annual fee. The legacy I had left behind with my one-person audience was certainly valuable to them: it showed them how they could keep hold of a client who had given them 20 years of business.

Blurring

Another challenge that I often get from clients is something along the following lines:

'Sometimes, isn't the Micro-Statement merely a Statement of what I want the Finishing Position to be?'

I agree that it could be … *if it isn't a very good Micro-Statement*. An extreme Statement of that point of view might be:

'Surely, if I want to convince them that we need to recruit more staff in Bristol, my Micro-Statement should just be, "we need to recruit more staff in Bristol".'

My answer to that is that the Micro-Statement really should have the spice and colour that drives the audience *towards* the Finishing Position, rather than just being a flat announcement of that position. So, a Micro-Statement that does the job rather better in this instance might be:

'If we don't do something to relieve the workload of our Bristol team, there is a danger that many of our best people will leave us and our West Country operation will implode.'

I suggest that the words in the Micro-Statement above are rather more likely to have the right persuasive effect than a flat Statement of the desired Finishing Position. If you find that your Micro-Statement is merely a vanilla paraphrased of the desired Finishing Position, then you have simply not done enough work on it.

A Listening Device

I have already mentioned that I first started to use immediate encapsulation as a way of appreciating speeches rather than writing them. I suggest that you can also use the concept as a way of making your own experience as an audience member more useful and enjoyable.

The vast majority of the speakers that you hear will not be familiar with the idea of a Micro-Statement, but you can still use the concept as a listening-lens through which you can focus what they are saying. All you have to do is ask yourself the question: If it was me making that speech, what would be the Micro-Statement that I would be trying to leave behind?

You will find that your ability do to this will be directly proportional to the quality of the speech that you are listening to. The better the speech, the easier it will be for you to encapsulate and pass on the key material to other people. On the other hand, some speeches are so confused, meandering and verbose that it is impossible for even the keenest Micro-Statement enthusiast to capture something worthwhile.

Every time you use the concept of a Micro-Statement as a listening tool, it will strengthen your ability and inclination to use it as a *preparation* tool.

If the answer to question 5 of the Action Steps below is 'yes', you are ready to move on to the next stage: using the Micro-Statement as the engine to drive the rest of the presentation creation process.

Action Steps: Making the Statement

1. Write down, in one sentence, what you want the audience to remember above all else.

2. Make certain that you are creating something that is significantly useful to the listener(s).

3. Ensure that the Statement assertively persuades the audience to adopt the desired Finishing Position.

4. Hone the phrasing so that it is as memorable and concise as possible.

5. Having gone through the four steps above, stare coldly at the finished product and ask yourself, 'if the only thing that the audience remembered was this Micro-Statement, would that be a good enough result?'

Chapter 4

HARDCORE CONTENT

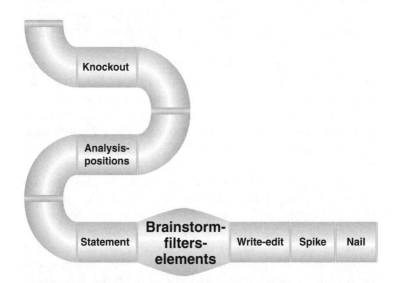

The Micro-Statement is the foundation on which your content will be built. Everything that you eventually say in front of the audience should be calculated to convince them to accept and act on the Micro-Statement. This is why you should literally never lose sight of it.

It will probably also serve the function of being the jewel that shines out from inside the presentation: the most valuable treasure that is revealed by your spoken words. The Micro-Statement can be the gift that you want the audience to take home with them.

Take a sheet of A4, turn it sideways and draw an oval in the middle of the page. Write out your Micro-Statement in the middle of the oval. Then add on some legs around the body, so that it looks like a very fat centipede. You are going to use this strange creature as a brainstorming device. It should look a bit like the example in the Preparation Pipeline Summary at the end of the book.

Now … *brainstorm* around the Micro-Statement. Think about all the possible bits of material that you might conceivably use to support the Micro-Statement. This might include facts, statistics, percentages, anecdotes, customer experiences, testimonials, jokes, blunt statements of personal opinion … and many other things. The idea is to be *inclusive* rather than *ex*clusive at this stage.

Do not disturb the flow of the ideas by trying to edit any of them. Squeeze everything out of your head that just might possibly be used as presentation content. As each piece of material occurs to you, write it out in summary, or just as a heading, at the end of one of the creature's legs. You may end up using all the legs, so that you have to add on more.

The Micro-Statement is thus constantly close to the centre of your vision. At the same time, this method (using the legs as locations to jot down possible material) forces you to carry out the brainstorming process in a non-hierarchical way. If the items were written out as a conventional top-to-bottom list, it is inevitable that the candidate material nearest to the top of the list would receive preferential treatment. When the material is placed around the legs it will all have the same visual status. This means that stuff that you thought of relatively late in the brainstorming process has a fair chance of being considered properly instead of automatically being seen as less important.

I strongly recommend that you carry out this exercise on paper, rather than being tied to the tidy purity of a screen. You must feel free to scribble without thought for grammar, spelling or neatness. Pen and paper will liberate your thoughts.

Let's take the example of the 'Lazerforce' presentation to golfers from the previous chapter. Here is a reminder of the Micro-Statement:

'This the right club for you because it allows you to hit the ball the longest possible distance in a straight line, at the most competitive price.'

If I brainstormed possible content, using that Micro-Statement as a stimulus, this is what I might come up with:

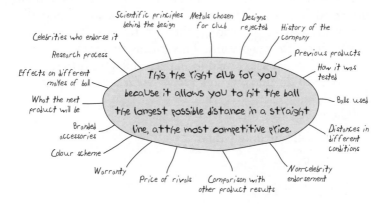

These headings are all reasonable preliminary candidates for inclusion in the final presentation.

Brainstorming should be seen as a finite process. By that I mean that you should allocate a specific period of time for it to be completed. After that period of time has elapsed, be ruthless with yourself: make the conscious decision that no more new material will be considered for conclusion after that point ... unless you experience an extraordinary flash of inspiration.

If you have an hour in which to do all your preparation, I suggest that you spend no more than 15 minutes of brainstorming. This is how long it took to create the example above. However, I am not going to suggest that you allocate time based on a fixed percentage. You may have the sort of mind that works best by attacking the problem at several sittings on separate days. Many people prefer to get the brainstorming done in one purgative mega-session.

On the other hand, I took part in the brainstorming for Michael Howard's speech at the 2004 British Conservative Party Conference. This part of the preparation process took three months!

In the Lazerforce brainstorm above, there is far more material than you could possibly include in the final presentation. The audience would feel bombarded rather than informed. The sheer volume of information would actually get in the way of persuading them to travel to the Finishing Position that you want. This means that your next job is to cut the material down to manageable proportions. You are going to do this by using *filters and testing the emotional punch.*

There are three filters that you can use:

1. The Micro-Statement

2. The Factual Filter

3. The Anti-Filter

Each filter is used in a slightly different way.

The Micro-Statement Filter

Of course, there should already be nothing attached to the legs of the creature that does not support the Micro-Statement. But it is possible that you might have come up with a few things that are merely interesting facts *relating to* the Micro-Statement. For instance, the new clothing range related to the Lazerforce Golf Club may be very attractive and of some general interest, but mentioning it in the actual presentation does not significantly support the core contention of the Micro-Statement.

So ... let's look at the creature's legs and eliminate those headings which have only a peripheral relationship to what you want the audience to take away with them. The only headings that should survive are the one that profoundly strengthen the argument you are projecting. In the Brainstorm Centipede below, I have highlighted in bold those headings that do not make it through the Micro-Statement filter:

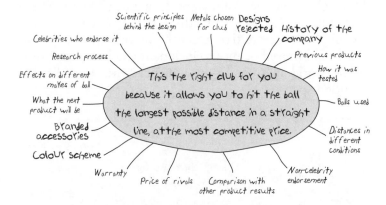

Here is my reasoning for each rejection:

- The audience will only be interested in the design that is actually being offered to them, not the ones that have been rejected.
- I feel that the glorious history of the company will not be a factor in them working out whether the current range provide what they need.
- Both the colour scheme of the club and the related clothing range certainly do not relate to the ball-striking effectiveness of the product.

The 17 original headings are thus reduced to 13.
You are then ready to move on to the Factual Filter.

The Factual Filter

This filter involves the use of three key phrases:

- Nice to know
- Should know
- Must know

Each phrase is a possible description of each individual piece of material that remains at the end of the creature's legs.

'Nice to know' material should be easy to identify. Although it has successfully got through the Micro-Statement filter, it is clearly something that is not vital to the overall effect you are trying to achieve. It is the fluffy stuff that would indeed be nice to include if you had all the time in the world in front of an audience with an unlimited attention span.

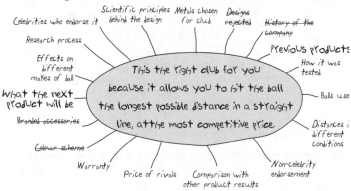

Here is my reasoning for each rejection (highlighted in bold):

- Previous products do not relate to the audience's immediate concerns, i.e. how their golf games can almost automatically be improved by a purchase of what is available *now*.
- Ditto future planned products.

The 13 edited headings are thus further reduced to 11.

You are then ready to move on to the 'should know' test.

The word 'should' is often preceded by the word 'maybe' … as in '*Maybe* the audience should be told some of the details of the research process involved in the creation of the club.' My own judgement is that this is a detail too far, even for an audience of keen golfers. I also feel that exploring the differences in the distances achieved with different makes and types of golf ball will not be something that helps to keep the audience's attention. They are golfers, not golf geeks.

I also feel that the performance of the club in different terrains and weather conditions may only be of peripheral interests, so this heading does not quite make the cut.

This is the most difficult call that you will have to make while using the factual filter. There is a very thin borderline between what should be eliminated and what survives (see highlights in bold). You will sometimes have the room to include the 'Should Knows'. You will only get the knack of it by going through this mental discipline for several presentations over a period of time.

You should now be left with material with is 'must know'.

Once all the 'Nice to knows' and the vast majority of the 'Should knows' have been crossed out, you are left with the non-negotiable items: the stuff that you really want the audience to walk away with and remember ... and perhaps tell other people about. Here is the list of headings we are left with (in bold):

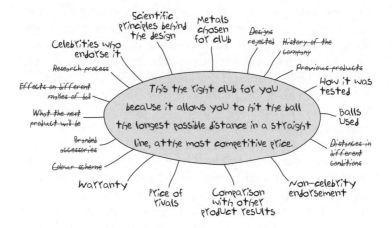

You are now ready to consider the most touchy-feely part of content filtration: the **Anti-Filter**.

The Anti-Filter

As a successful presenter you should aspire to penetrate the emotional depths of the audience.

This may mean reinstating material that you have just discarded in the process of filtration above. This is because your words will gain more resonance with the audience if they play to the audience's **Terrors** and **Triumphs**. The Factual Filter cannot fully cater for this aspect of the audience: only intuition and research can work this angle.

So ... with this in mind, look again at *every* heading on the original Brainstorm Centipede, even the ones that did not survive after you have used the first two filters.

What might they be afraid of?

Consider whether any of the headings may help the audience to combat any terrors they might have ... things that they are scared of in this context.

Returning to our example used above, lets say that nearly all the golfers I am speaking to are members of a golf club which prides itself on the vast array of conditions of each of its 18 holes. It is a very distinctive course which manages to combine the characteristics of coastal, parkland and mountain topography. Golfers are therefore faced many different challenges. Because of this, one of the things my audience will definitely worry about is how the club will perform in different conditions. Look again at the original headings listed earlier. The heading that *now* stands out as something that is necessary for the presentation's success is the one about the club's performance in different weathers and terrains (originally discarded at the Should Know stage).

So ... application of the Anti-Filter means that this heading is saved from the content scrap heap and may well make it into the final presentation.

As a further illustration, I now suggest that we take a momentary detour away from the golf course into a more corporate scenario. Let's say you are proposing to your colleagues that your company gets involved in a business venture in Rome. 'Italian Bankruptcy Legislation' is one of the headings that did not make it through the first two filters. But then you remember that the company was involved in another Italian Job several years ago in which their partners went but they lost a great deal of money. They will certainly be frightened of a repeat performance. Your description of the turgid vagaries of Italian Law therefore scrapes back into the mix after all.

Good vibrations?

We should now look at all the headings and see whether any of them relate to something that has worked so well for this audience before that it could be considered a triumph. An example might be a previous product of this company (as mentioned in one of the discarded headings). If this older type of product has a reputation for being extremely useful in ever-changing golfing circumstances, then a reference to it during the presentation may help the audience to feel again an emotional triumph. This positive feeling might then be transferred to the current product, thus supporting the Micro-Statement and helping to propel the audience to the desired Finishing Position.

However, I happen to know that the old product was merely an adequate one and certainly did not have a triumphant reputation ... so the Anti-Filter does not save this heading and it remains on the scrap heap.

But let me give you a positive example, this time in a political context. Let's say you are a candidate preparing a speech to an audience of supporters in a particular town in the build-up to a General Election. Using the Micro-Statement and Factual Filters, you may have decided that the headings you want to focus on are Cutting the Deficit, Reducing Waste and Eliminating Poverty. The heading Looking After Troops didn't quite manage to survive. However, you then look at your headings again through the Anti-Filter of Terrors and Triumphs. This reminds you that this town's local regiment has just returned home after a tough, but successful deployment abroad. It is therefore vital that you acknowledge this Triumph if you are to persuade the audience that you and your Party really understand their needs.

Filter Use Summary

The Anti-Filter should not be applied with the binary brutality of the Factual Filter. Although we certainly believe that concern for audience needs must shine throughout the presentation, references to Terrors and Triumphs should be seen as valuable, but not vital, added extras. If you are under extreme time pressure, you should spend only a relatively short period on considering the emotional aspect of the subject.

Apply the Micro-Statement and Factual Filters with savage ruthlessness.

Consider the Anti-filter as a desirable bonus ... if you have time.

I have described the filtering process as though it is linear: Micro-Statement filter, then Factual filter, then Anti-filter. However, in reality, you will probably need to use the filters in a circular fashion, going back over them more than once to make sure that you have been thorough enough.

From Filtering to Grouping

The original brainstorm example above has 18 legs, each with a heading describing possible content that the presenter is thinking of including.

You may well have 18 points you want to include. They may all be very important. But the chances of 18 points being absorbed and acted on are very slim indeed. As an experiment, try starting off a presentation with the words:

'I have 18 topics I would like to cover today ...'

The most prevalent expression you then see on the faces of the audience is likely to be one of anger or despair. Make sure you have locked the exits.

If 18 headings are too many, how many *should* you have?

The ideal number is probably three. For some reason, the human mind feels very comfortable with groups of three. It seems as though lists of three items are memorable, even when the words in the list are not very striking in themselves:

'Friends, Romans, Countrymen ...'

'Veni, Vidi, Vici' (it works in Latin, too)

'Blood, Sweat and Tears'

Churchill *actually* said 'Blood, sweat, *toil* and tears'. But most people have forgotten the toil because a list of three is easier to remember.

I accept that three may seem like a very small number of headings for an important presentation. But think back to the last big speech or presentation that you heard. Can you remember more headings than that from it? Can you even remember three? Or anything remotely approaching a Micro-Statement?

If you manage to get your next audience to remember your Micro-Statement and three headings that support it, you will have done better than 99% of other presenters.

Nevertheless, it may be the case that, despite the most vigorous use of the filters you just can't get the headings down to three. Well, I reluctantly concede that you can probably get away with as many as five headings, and still have a chance of the audience absorbing them if your writing is really tight. You should consider five as an absolute maximum, because audience memory capacity seems to coincide with the number of fingers on the human hand.

Grouping

If you really do have 17 points that you really do need to cover (God help the audience), then do your best to *group* them. This is the list of nine headings you are left with after applying all three filters mentioned earlier:

- Celebrities who endorse it.
- Scientific principles behind the design.
- Metals chosen for club.
- How it was tested.
- Distances in different conditions.
- Non-celebrity endorsement.
- Comparison with other product results.
- Price of rivals.
- Warranty.

Let's now consider whether we can divide these into three groups:

- Scientific principles behind the design.
- Metals chosen for club.
- How it was tested.

- Distances in different conditions.
- Comparison with other product results.
- Price of rivals.
- Warranty.

- Non-celebrity endorsement.
- Celebrities who endorse it.

These three groups of headings can then be *chunked* together under three super-headings:

1. The Technology.

2. The Performance.

3. The Testimonials.

Audiences do not like having to work hard. Grouping and chunking makes their life just a little bit easier – at least for the duration of your presentation. And because it helps you to clarify and remember the core content of your presentation, it will also make *your* life easier.

The Clanger Check

A Clanger is a piece of information that seems to help you to project the Micro-Message, but after further thought, usually with the help of trusted colleagues, it becomes clear that it may well have the opposite effect. This is the sort of scenario where you show someone your list of proba-ble headings and they say, 'What???!!!! Are you completely bonkers? If you talk about that, you've got no chance of persuading them!'

One of my corporate clients was recently planning a presentation that was intended to motivate and inspire his team to even greater success. He had carefully gone through all the filters. One of the surviving headings was 'The Denver Project'. He intended to spend a large proportion of his speaking time dealing with the lessons that could be drawn from the project. The unfortunate thing was that this particular venture had been an utter disaster, during the course of which several people had lost a great deal of credibility. The upside of lessons learned was far outweighed by the de-motivating downside of exhuming this corporate corpse and dissecting in front of an audience who were heartily sick of it. Just to squeeze as much out of this metaphor as possible, the smell of decay would certainly have driven his audience *away* from the desired Finishing Position.

It was only when I pointed out this potential clanger that he decided to put the Denver Project back into the grave where it belonged.

So, if you have the time and the colleagues available, ask them to look at your final list of content to make sure that you don't spend a lot of time developing the detail of something that will be harmful to your presentational purpose.

The term I use for the super-headings created above is **Key Elements**, because they are the key to unlocking the real value of the Micro-Statement. It is those Key Elements which become the Hardcore Content after which this chapter is named.

After you have gone through the sequence summarized in the following Action Steps, it is time to write the content which will become the flesh on the bones of the Key Elements.

Action Steps

1. Write out your Micro-Statement in the middle of a Centipede.

2. Brainstorm all the headings that could possibly flow from the Micro-Statement.

3. Apply the Micro-Statement Filter, so that only headings that profoundly support the Micro-Statement remain.

4. Apply the Factual Filter, so that only must-know headings remain.

5. Apply the Anti-filter, so that Terrors and Triumphs are covered.

6. Group headings together, so that they become Key Elements.

7. Check for Clangers.

CHAPTER 5

WRITE IT, READ IT, EDIT

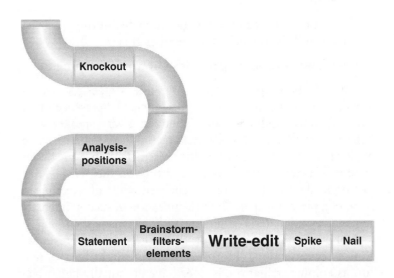

Once you have survived the creative heat from the process outlined in Chapter 3, you will have created a carefully phrased Micro-Statement and probably between three and five key elements which support it.

At this stage, your key elements are probably little more than rough notes. There is still a lot of work to do before you can safely feel that your spoken content has been properly prepared. We will deal with your vital opening and closing words in the next chapter, but now it is time to put some wholesome and fulfilling flesh on to the main body of the presentation. You must make the effort to expand on what you already have.

Write it Out

My clients often come out with the following sort of justification for *not* really doing this properly:

'A few rough notes are all I need to prepare. I don't actually need to write out my presentation because I am confident that I will find the right words when I am in front of the audience.'

I accept that most presenters never write out their presentations in full. Nevertheless, remember this:

If it's not worth writing out, it's not worth listening to.

You will think up your best material in a quiet room with a pen, paper and (sometimes) a computer. The presence of an audience only inhibits creative thought. Every speaker who believes that they are at their best creating new material while a lot of people are staring at them is in fact an even better creator of material when they are sitting on their own. They just don't like the sheer, non-adrenalized effort of sweating in front of a piece of paper. Their relative level of success in creating and saying material simultaneously has made them lazy.

Nobody *enjoys* writing out the words of the presentation. I certainly don't. However, while it might be as much fun as colonic irrigation, it does have an equally beneficial purgative effect. In going through the act of clearing out the blockage of ill-defined thoughts, you will be forced to eliminate all the words and sentences that just don't work. Moreover, it is only when you see them on paper or screen that you can really start to work out which words really *do* work. You can read and re-read them. Insert a word here; chop out a sentence there. You can fuss, worry and agonise. It is well worth the effort of making your words battle-ready.

I am not suggesting that you use the same process as when you used to write essays for exams. In those days, you probably thought in terms of correct grammar, sentences with verbs in the appropriate tense and precise punctuation. Or at least you did if you went to a half-decent school.

You probably also wrote your essays in silence … because you were writing them for someone who would also read them in silence. When you write out the words of a presentation, you should say them out loud and then write them down. This means that you have a pretty good idea of whether they work or not before they even hit the page. In this way, the words you create will be born out loud, have a temporary childhood on screen or paper and eventually come to active maturity while coming out of your mouth again.

This word-growth sequence is not meant to be totally smooth. At times, you will find yourself thinking:

> 'Wait a minute … this just doesn't look right … and it certainly doesn't sound right … I've put in some irrelevant stuff … and left out something crucial!'

This is not a negative thought. It is a constructive thought. It encourages you to do something about the situation. It is also fine to have this thought any time up to the last few minutes before your presentation.

Warning: if you have that thought during the presentation, it is simply too late. The adjustments you make on your feet will never be as good as the ones you could have calculated in advance.

So …. don't be lazy. Don't just rough it out. WRITE it out.

I know what I have just proposed will meet a lot of resistance. The idea of writing out the words of the presentation is an unpopular one. Here is the kind of typical reaction I hear all the time from new clients:

> 'I can't possibly do that … you just don't realize how busy I am. I don't have time to waste on actually writing

the thing verbatim. I barely have the time to get my slides together.'

They are right to feel the pressure on their time. They are wrong to thing that comprehensive preparation is a *waste* of that time.

Writing it out has several advantages:

1. **You are more likely to be able to think effectively in front of a screen or a piece of paper than in front of an audience.** The live energy of the occasion itself should stimulate your *performance*, but it will not stimulate your *creativity*. Most normal people come up with their best stuff in an atmosphere of calm reflection, well in advance of the presentation itself.

2. **Faulty ideas are best exposed on paper or screen.** You may well think that the concepts in your head are totally clear and credible, but this could be an illusion. It is difficult to think about them objectively unless you can *see* them put into words.

3. **Complexity kills communication.** It can confuse your audience and thus they are less likely to absorb and agree with your Micro-Statement. To be effective, the presentation structure must essentially be simple and *linear*. You can only test your script for effective simplicity if you can see it written down.

Still not convinced? You need to be. Writing it out is not a luxury. Read on.

Once you have put it on paper you can decide upon the best method of delivery. Do you need a full script that you put on auto-cue? Would abbreviated notes to use as an aide memoir be a better option? Whatever you decide, the end result will be much better if you have gone to the trouble of writing out a full script.

In doing so you will:

- force yourself to decide on the best order for the material;
- spot where repetition is necessary and where it is harmful;
- eliminate clichés and inappropriate jargon;
- cross check content with the Micro-Statement;
- be able to shape the overall flow and improve the tone.

The good news is that I really do not want you to rebel against the Bare Knuckle method just because you dread the agony of writing out every single word that you intend to say.

If you did try to write everything out, you would actually be writing out a *script*. A script is something that the deliverer is expected to stick to religiously, like an actor saying the words that have been provided by a playwright.

But presenting is very definitely not a form of acting. It *is* a performance ... but one where you are always yourself rather than pretending to be a character that has been created by someone else. And when you are being yourself, you simply *cannot* stick religiously to the words typed on your computer because that would feel and sound un-natural.

So, instead of writing out a verbatim script, I urge you to write a Baseline Text instead.

A **Baseline Text** is a version of the speech which contains all the key phrases that you will actually use on the day. It will probably contain about 70% of the words of your full speech. This allows you to get all the really important stuff on screen or paper, but without creating a straightjacket of words that you are trapped inside no matter what.

If you have been using pen and paper in the process up to this point, now is the time to move to your computer.

Technology can greatly ease the pain of squeezing out the best words. Even the most basic laptops these days are able to run excellent voice recognition software that enables you to talk your way onto the screen. After a little practice, you will find that it speeds up your thinking quite considerably. Of course, I have nothing but admiration for people who learned how to type properly early on in their working or school lives. But for those of us who stumble through the written word enslaved on the keyboard by a barely adequate two-finger twitch, voice recognition is profoundly liberating.

Read it for Sense

Look, I do realize that the chances of you following my next bit of advice are very slim. It would be easy to skip it and go on to the next stage....but I am going to say it anyway.

Read through the Baseline Text twice to make sure that it all makes sense.

I know that you will think that this is tedious and you just don't have enough time in your day. But please try it for me. You will sometimes be amazed by the sheer gibberish that you were certain was cogent genius at the time you first wrote it out.

I am now going to annoy you even more. Having persuaded you to put so much effort into expanding and reading through your key elements, I am now urge you to reduce your word count with some shrewd editing.

Edit for Impact

The most powerful weapon on your computer is the delete key. It allows you to cleanly eliminate unwanted words without the untidy unpleasantness of crossings-out on a piece of paper. Cutting-and-pasting can also become an absolute joy when you realize that some of your otherwise excellent words are simply in the wrong place.

Resist the desire to tell all. This requires courage and focus. Some presenters seem to have taken truth serum which forces them to blurt out everything ... as though only a full confession will end the threat of torture. Sadly, this attitude leads to *the audience* being tortured instead.

Ironically, although many people *do* write a script for their speech, they put all that effort to waste *by not saying it out loud* until the actual performance of the presentation itself! This is most often the cause of those butt-clenchingly embarrassing moments for the audience as they watch you struggling to deliver. And I'm not sure which is the worse position to be in; the shoes of the presenter or the fidgeting audience.

None of the following presentational phenomena are enjoyable:

- Sentences that continue for paragraphs or even pages without end or even punctuation.

- Condescending questions that suddenly sound absurd when spoken out loud, like '*What do we mean by leadership?*'

- Filler words and phrases that work as padding on paper but sound thin when presented:

  'I don't know if you saw ...'

  (Does it really matter if they saw it and if they did, what difference does it make?)

  'I think you will agree that ...'

  (are you certain that they all would?)

  'An objective that is close to all our hearts'

  (what good objective is *not* close to anyone's heart?)

- Complex concepts that, when available to a reader to reread are acceptable, but which are impossible to follow in the hear-it-once environment of presentation:

  '... developing the desire to understand and fix things into the ability to diagnose and repair an elusive intermittent electrical fault using the latest equipment, documentation and support facilities.'

- Tricky words or sequences of words that would stand little chance of being delivered under pressure.

- Colloquial phrases that, when delivered in a business context, sound at best cheesy and at worst laughable:

  'This will really get your pulse racing ....'

- Horrible corporate clichés that should only be said when deliberately playing Bullshit Bingo. Because, when the going gets tough, the weak use clichés:

  'The only constant is change'

  (Translation: If you don't perform we sack you)

  'This is a real win-win situation'.

  (Twice as much cliché for the price of one).

  'This is not a problem: it's an opportunity'.

  (Our results are disastrous, but I'm desperately trying to sound positive).

  'We are customer-focused and market-driven'.

  (Some consultant told us we should pretend to be).

  'There are no easy answers'.

  (We need more consultants).

  'The future of the company depends on you'.

  (Because we can't afford to make you all redundant).

Structure

When we are reading a document, we have the option of going back and re-reading a section to make sure that we understand it. An audience does not have this option.

If an audience has to work hard to follow the flow, it saps a lot of their collective energy: energy which you want them to use for absorbing your Micro-Statement. Audiences are turned off by hard work. Make it easy for them. Use a straightforward structure.

The structure has to be simple enough to be:

(a)   easy to follow;

(b)   easy to remember;

(c)   easy to communicate to someone else.

An audience likes to feel that a presenter has appropriate authority – about his subject and about the way he communicates it. An effective presenter, therefore, is an effective leader. But there is a fine line between leading and patronising. Remember, the audience needs to make the journey *with* you.

You don't want the journey to be a magical mystery tour. You don't want anyone listening to you to be thinking:

'There are some good ideas here, but I can't quite see what he is really driving at'

But, on the other hand, you don't want to reveal too much too soon:

'He's told us he's going to be dealing with Sales in Bristol, Marketing in Birmingham and Costs in Sheffield ... so I'm not going to bother listening to the Bristol and Birmingham stuff because I'm only interested in Sheffield.'

The 'Sheffield' example above is an excellent illustration of the perils of the old and clichéd 'Tell them' theory, which goes as follows:

Tell them what you are going to tell them.

Tell them.

Tell them what you have told them.

What that really means is:

Tell them that you're going to be patronizing.

BE patronizing.

Then tell them what the word *'patronizing'* really means.

The 'Tell them' theory works very well for nursery teachers. For anyone else, it is boring, bland and out of date.

Of course, a good structure should give the presentation to give a strong indication of how those listening are going to get to the Finishing Position. But it must do this without becoming too predictable. The old style 'Tell them' presenter might use the following sort of phrasing for a presentation about the subject matter of the costs presentation above:

'Good morning, ladies and gentlemen. It's a great privilege for me to be allowed the opportunity to ...

(lots more yawning platitudes)

... today I'm going to cover Sales in Bristol and Marketing in Birmingham before going on to spend a few minutes discussing Costs in Sheffield. But first of all, let me tell you a bit about the background ...'

This presentation is clearly going to be an adrenalin-free zone. The audience has no doubt about where they are going. But they also have no doubt that they are going to be bored.

The Bare-Knuckle Presenter would start with something much sharper (as you will discover in the next chapter).

Don't force the audience to work out your structure. Make it clear enough so that they can relax into your content. Give them strong leadership, and they will follow you along your presentational route.

Elsinore or Hollywood?

This is what happened in *Hamlet*:

Hamlet is upset because his Dad has died, and his Mum has married the bloke that Hamlet thinks might have killed him.

Hamlet wonders what to do.

He decides to pretend to be mad and dumps his girlfriend, who then kills herself.

Hamlet then kills some other old bloke, then the old bloke's son and then his mother's new husband and is then killed himself.

The Complete Shakespeare Company managed to tell the story in 12 words:

'Look … a ghost!'

'To be or not to be.'

'The rest is silence.'

OK, Shakespeare's original four-hour version is probably a bit better.

Most people in the 21st century already know some version of the story before they go and see an actual production of Hamlet. That was not the case in Shakespeare's time. Although there would of course have been some gossip percolating about the plot, the majority of any given audience would be ignorant about the flow of events before walking into the theatre. They were experiencing the story for the first time as it happened in front of them.

But even the most highly educated and intelligent audience members would not be able to grasp all the intricate themes blended into the text. That is why billions of words have been written about the play over the last 300 years. No audience can possibly absorb it all the first time.

So…a Shakespearean Tragedy is a poor model for business presentation.

Here is what will happen in the next James Bond film:

James works for British Intelligence.

An Evil Villain wants to do Something Very Bad.

James has casual sex and kills him.

Every member of every cinema audience will know that this is what is going to happen, long before they even leave home that night. But they also know that they are still going to like the explosions, the killing and the special effects. And the casual sex. They are just there to enjoy the experience.

They will not worry about being unable to grasp the intricate themes, because there aren't any. Very few PhD theses have been written about the plot lines of Goldfinger.

An audience can absorb the structure and the meaning of it all the first time, because there is almost nothing to absorb.

A good Bare Knuckle business presentation lies somewhere between William Shakespeare and James Bond.

It cannot just be an enjoyable experience. It must have a worthwhile Micro-Statement, together with sharp supporting content, that can be absorbed the first time it is heard. There can be nothing hidden inside an intricate structure.

The structure must have 007 simplicity, rather than Hamlet complexity.

Other books on the art of presentation spend a lot of time analyzing several possible structures that could be used in presentations. That is not Bare Knuckle Presenting. It is academic navel gazing.

Imagine that I have magically appeared in front of you now. I am wearing the clothes of a Presentation Dictator. I have come to make the following declaration:

There can be only one type of presentation structure.

This is it, the Bare Knuckle Structure:

First Spike

Micro-Statement

Key Element 1

Element 2

Element 3

More Elements, if necessary

Possible echo of Micro-Statement

Possible Summary

End Spike

What is meant by the terms 'First Spike' and 'End Spike' will be explained in the next chapter. Every presentation you will ever do can use this structure. It is simple, adaptable and transparent. It is easy to follow and easy to tell someone else about.

In summary:

Say it, support it, shut it.

Order of Elements

Sometimes it will be obvious that you should order the elements in a chronological sequence that follows the narrative story you need to tell, i.e. past, present, future. However, this may come across as very bland and predictable. Let's say that the three key elements of your presentation are:

- Historical background to the problem.
- Current challenge.
- The solution.

It may seem obvious that the correct order for these elements should be precisely that above. However, I have seen countless eyes glaze over at the words, 'before I tell you about the current situation and what we are going to do about it, I would just like to tell you a little bit about the background …'

Hopefully you will have gone through a rigorous filtering process before deciding that the historical background is a must-know. But even if it is as necessary as you believe, it is unlikely to be the part of the presentation that your audience is burning to hear.

I strongly suggest that you might want to tinker with the order AND the division of material in the key elements, so that the sequence more accurately reflects the likely lusts of the audience:

- Tight summary of solution.
- Historical background.
- Current challenge.
- Detail of solution.

This order achieves the double-hit of giving the audience some immediate satisfaction, while at the same time encouraging them to look forward to more.

Any questions?

'Should the Micro-Statement always be so close to the beginning?'

In the vast majority of presentations, yes. An audience is always at its most receptive at the start. If you state your Micro-Statement as soon as possible, then you know that you will definitely have said the most important thing, even if you have to finish early for some reason.

Always bear in mind that the 21st century audience is an impatient one. In all my years of experience, I have never watched a presentation where I felt that the presenter got to their Micro-Statement too soon. I have seen plenty where it was just too late.

However, especially in long presentations, there is a strong possibility that you should remind them of the Micro-Statement somewhere close to the end. If possible, avoid repeating exactly the same words. An echo, rather than a straight repeat is what you should aim for.

For instance, remember the Micro-Statement of the Lazerforce presentation:

'The Lazerforce range is the right range of clubs for you because it allows you to hit the ball the longest possible distance, in a straight line, at the most competitive price.'

The final echo of this might be:

'I am certain that the distance and accuracy that you will get from these clubs will more than justify the price you have paid.'

Another common challenge I hear is:

'But if they are likely to be against me, isn't there a risk that saying the Micro-Statement right away will turn them off completely when I've hardly begun?'

Yes, occasionally you have to adapt to the needs of an antagonistic audience. Let's say that your detailed audience analysis has revealed that they may be aggressively unsympathetic to your Micro-Statement. After careful consideration, you may decide that you need to take them through your supporting arguments before you hit them with the Micro-Statement. There is a reasonable chance that they will feel less ill disposed towards your crown jewel if it is justified and *then* revealed.

If you have followed the advice summarized in the Action Steps below, you should have created a Baseline Text that consists of about three quarters of the words that you will actually say on the day.

The next chapter will help you decide on the exact words that you will use to begin and end the presentation.

Action Steps

1. Taking each Key Element heading separately, decide on the exact words that you actually want to say in the final presentation which support that heading, preferably by talking directly to your computer.

2. Remember that you only need to capture about 75% of the words you are saying, ensuring that you have captured the crucial phrases verbatim.

3. Edit to eliminate:

   Long sentences

   Filler Phrases

   Over-Complex statements

   Unsayable phrases

   Trite colloquialism

   Tired clichés

4. Consider the most appealing order for the Key Elements, which is not necessarily chronological.

5. Place the Elements together in a Bare Knuckle Structure.

CHAPTER 6

FROM FAMOUS FIRST WORDS ...

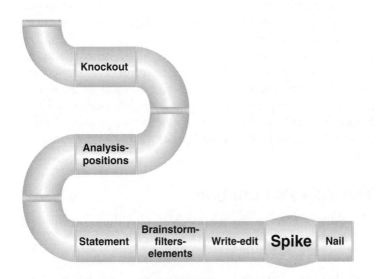

The two most important sentences in any presentation are the first and the last.

Beginning

An audience makes a decision about whether your presentation is worth listening to within the first few seconds. This is why you have to get to the point immediately.

The audience will always be at their most receptive right at the start. Take ruthless advantage of this. Grab their attention immediately by telling them something that snaps them away from their comfort zone. It must be striking enough to make them decide to take the action of listening. They should be propelled into thinking:

> 'Hey, this presenter isn't wasting any time. I must listen; otherwise I might miss something I need to hear.'

They may disagree with your first words but that is a risk you should be prepared to take. It is actually far more risky to be bland. Blandness is something that they have been bored by many times before. The very first sentence you say must be bold ... strong enough to give the audience a jolt that interrupts their cozy pattern of thinking. It must have an edge hard enough to cut into the audience consciousness. I call this device a **Spike**. For the sake of total clarity, whenever this device is used as an opening gambit in a presentation, you could also call it a **First Spike**. You will find that I alternate between using Spike, First Spike (and indeed **End Spike**) throughout the rest of the book.

The Spike's Function

The Spike has to be sharp enough to turn them on without pissing them off.

Here are some examples:

Audience: Potential corporate sponsors of charity
Speaker: Director of Charity

'80% of the world's resources are used by 20% of the world's population. There is plenty to go around. The

problem is unfair distribution and we are the only charity who can change this.'

Audience: City investors
Speaker: CEO of a Telecoms Company

'Half the population of the world has never made or received a phone call.'

'Telecommunications is still in the first stage of Global growth ... and now European Deregulation has given our company access to a 25 billion dollar marketplace.'

Or they can be slightly wordier:

Audience: UK Independent Financial Advisers, driven by money-making opportunities, hard nosed, cynical and rather disinterested
Speaker: Marketing Director of a Life Insurer

'Car companies rave about ABS, safety glass and airbags.'

'Home Security Suppliers recommend alarms, locks and light sensors.'

'High Street chemists have a one-size-fits-all solution in a variety of colours and flavours.'

'I am talking about PROTECTION.'

All of these examples cut straight through to what the audience really needs to hear. The presentation is already flying.

You don't have time to be a jumbo jet, lumbering down the runway before eventually gathering enough speed to get in the air. You should be like a Hawker Harrier fighter, jumping straight off the ground, ready for combat. The first few sentences need to be a vertical take-off.

Nobody really enjoys being kept in suspense for long, because it quickly becomes tedious. Your first words should open up the audience to the information you are about to give them.

The Spike can also make your point of view immediately obvious:

Audience: Councillors, journalists and local business-men

Speaker: Member of Greater London Assembly

'Motor car fumes are killing central London. Unless the Congestion Charge is immediately extended to Kensington, Chelsea and Fulham, every tree within the M25 will be dead.'

Great spikes spark questions
In the last example, several questions form immediately in the mind of the audience:

'What does he mean by killing?'

'Where does central London start?'

'Is he talking about company cars?'

'Where on earth does the research come from to back up a statement like that?'

The rest of the presentation should answer those questions.

You should not want the audience to be at ease
A relaxed audience is not necessarily an attentive audience.

Don't greet them with fluffy pleasantries. They will expect that. You can make a positive impact simply by leaving them out. I have never heard a presenter being criticized for getting to the point too quickly. The audience has not come to listen to a pleasant chat. There is no need to say 'Good morning'. If it is a small audience, you will probably have said that to most of them individually as they enter the room. If it is a large audience, the person introducing you will have said it. Indeed, *every* presenter at a large event will probably say it. Make sure you are the one that stands out because you do not waste any of the audience's time.

Remember that everyone in any audience will hear the words 'hello', or 'how are you doing?', or some variation, at least 100 times in a normal day. These phrases are really just background noise that does not take your communication further. The Bare-knuckle Presenter does not allow their impact to be diminished by background noise. In fact, these sorts of phrases are only words of comfort for the presenter rather than words of value for the audience.

You will not grab their attention by setting out an agenda
Agendas are a boring bit of housekeeping that should be done by someone else. If they don't know why you are there then there is something fundamentally wrong: the organizer has not done his job.

Taking time to tell them how long you will be speaking for is a waste of that time. The reference to time will cause the audience to concentrate on their watches rather than your content. If you make a prediction at the start about exactly how long you will speak for, there will always be a contingent who will feel betrayed if you go one second over.

It is how long your presentation *feels* to the audience that really counts, not how long it actually is.

Do not make excuses
Phrases such as, 'I was only told about this last night.' or I'm not much of a speaker or 'I don't have the right slides with me,' are, frankly, pathetic.

If you want to make an excuse for your inadequacy, the audience has an excuse for inattention. Any presenter who starts like this encourages nothing but contempt.

Starting with an apology does nothing for your credibility. The audience does not want to know what you cannot do; they want to know what you *can* do. They do not want to know why you were late or any other issues that you may have in your life – they have enough of their own. They would like your presentation to solve at least some of their problems immediately.

Do not start by asking the audience a question

Questions are dangerous for two reasons:

1. Somebody may answer.

2. Nobody may answer.

Let's say you ask a question that you hope will get some vocal response from somebody. If an audience member gives the obvious answer that everyone expects, that will be a very boring and predictable beginning.

If someone gives an answer you *don't* expect, then you have immediately lost control of your own presentation. You should not want them to expend mental energy on thinking of the answer to banal questions. All their energy should be focused on listening to *you* providing answers. Remember that forced audience participation is also the final hiding place of comedians on the edge of failure due to a lack of high-quality, pre-rehearsed material. Interaction is no replacement for content.

Another strong argument against asking a question is this: unless you are certain that the question is a hundred per cent relevant to a hundred per cent of the audience you can expect a significant dip in audience interest. You don't want them thinking their own questions: 'What's this got to do with me?', 'Doesn't he know? I thought it was the audience who is supposed to ask the questions?

The Bare-Knuckle Presenter only asks questions of audience members several hours or days before the presentation, when he is preparing his content. The presentation itself should not be asking questions. It should be providing *solutions.*

A question is a very cheap and over-used form of opening, endorsed by door-to-door brush salesmen across the globe:

'Good morning sir, have you ever thought that you would like more money, more time and more friends? I thought so. Well, if you buy just two of my wax impregnated brushes, your dreams will be answered.'

A particularly bland opening is:

'Hello and how is everyone this morning?'

These words expose the presenter to the strong possibility of a half-hearted reaction that demonstrates just how apathetic the audience feels towards the subject and the presenter. I recommend that you inquire after everyone's health as much as you like over coffee in the break, but when you are presenting you should just get on with delivering your carefully prepared material.

You should also eliminate rhetorical questions – where you do not expect to get an answer. They always sound pompous and outdated. Rhetoric was very popular in Ancient Greece. So was torture.

Do not get the audience to touch each other
This technique is adored by many American professional speakers. In Britain, the inclination to touch a complete stranger is considered a sign of weakness or criminal intent. If your audience members prefer listening to each other rather than to you, I suggest that you go home.

Do not open with a list of housekeeping
The link presenter or host should deal with housekeeping details at large events. *You* do not have time for them. They are more irrelevant background noise, getting in the way of the Micro-Message.

Do get them bolt upright
So the opening must be strong enough to give the audience a jolt. You must create a Spike that pricks the bubble of their pre-programmed thinking. You may even be able to raise a smile:

Audience: Communications Department of Asian
                    Motor Manufacturer
Speaker: Head of PR for their European Operation

'Icebergs are not a problem in this area of the Atlantic.

So said the Communications Director of the Titanic.

Such are the dangers of out-of-date information.'

It is even possible for a politician to successfully use humour in a Spike, something we were able to provide for Iain Duncan Smith when he spoke at the Institute of Directors annual dinner.

'Ladies and Gentlemen, this has been a tremendous day for me. The latest polls published by Mori and Gallup have confirmed that I have now managed to become the most popular Conservative leader since William Hague.'

Self-deprecation is a tool to be used sparingly in creating a spike. Mind you, when the line was actually delivered, there was a delicious momentary pause before the audience erupted with the realization that Iain was the *only* Conservative leader since William Hague.

A Spike can have an emotive aspect to it. I once spoke at a charity dinner where the speaker immediately preceding me was a senior executive from a Hospital that does some incredible work with tetraplegic patients. When I heard her very first words, I thought that she was going to trot out a sequence of bland pleasantries. I am delighted to say that I was totally wrong:

'Mister Chairman, many thanks for your hospitality. As it is St George's day, I am sure everyone particularly enjoyed the Roast Beef. But imagine how much less you would have enjoyed it if you were unable to move your arms or hold anything in your hands ... and every slice had to be cut up and placed in your mouth by someone else.'

'It is people with problems exactly like these that we help every day.'

Together with the rest of the audience, I was mesmerized.

Sharp, one-liner gags are also highly effective Spikes. If I know that the host of the dinner I am speaking has a more than moderately thick skin, I might use a line that looks like it is going to be a pleasantry but actually turns out to be anything but:

> *'Mister Chairman, I have been lucky enough to have been invited to some really tremendous dinners over the last few months, but I think I can safely say that your dinner tonight has certainly been, by a long chalk ... the most recent.'*

Whether it is funny or deadly serious, an effective Spike is the hard edge that cuts through all the fluff between you and your audience.

A few years ago, I had more credibility at the Criminal Bar than I do now. One day, I was defending a client on a Theft charge at Guildford Crown Court. He had been working as a labourer on a building site. He was accused of stealing a few bits of wood from the site.

When I say a few bits of wood, I mean a couple of lorry loads. His story was that he had just been doing what the foreman had told him to do. The foreman (who had pleaded guilty) had been doing it for months. My client said that he had no idea what the foreman was up to. He simply didn't realize that what they were doing could be seen as dishonest. He had merely been following orders. This is a defence that was made popular in Nuremberg a few years ago. Popular but ineffective.

As defence counsel, the only asset I had was that my client was very obviously very stupid indeed. I decided to create a spike that used this fact ruthlessly. I didn't cross-examine any of the prosecution witnesses. The only witness I called was the defendant himself so that the audience (i.e. the jury) could work out his IQ for themselves. The more he got torn apart in cross-examination by prosecution counsel, the better it was for me (kindness and compassion are not pre-requisites for the Criminal Bar).

My closing speech to the jury needed to have impact – right from the start. So this is what I opened with:

> *'Members of the jury – just look at the Defendant.*
>
> *Eloquent, Intellectual, Perspicacious – these are just three of the words that he can't even spell.*

He is thicker than any of the planks of wood on that building site.'

This was the prelude to me spending the next 20 minutes insulting my own client – something of a specialty of mine. The jury undoubtedly thought that I was arrogant, pompous and offensive – unusual for a barrister, I know. But I *had* given them a jolt. I had pushed them away from their assumption of guilt and I had started that process with the first 30 words of my speech.

They found him Not Guilty

And he now works on a building site somewhere near you.

The Ending

It would be a tragedy if all the focused work that you have put into preparing your presentation were to be ruined by a weak ending.

In the minds of the audience, a limp ending greatly detracts from what has gone before. Never forget that the last two sentences you say are the two most likely to be remembered ... so make sure that they are *worthy* of being remembered.

Try to think of the presentation as a wooden stake that needs to be equally sharp at both ends. If it is going to impale an oncoming enemy, the other end needs to have enough edge to be firmly embedded into the ground.

So make sure that the brilliance of your First Spike, Micro-Statement and Hard Core Content is matched by that of the End Spike.

Some of the most effective Finishes consist of a Summary and an End Spike. You can think of these as a one-two punch combination.

The Summary

As Churchill would have liked to have said, the summary is not the end, but it is the beginning of the end. It should come just before your very last words and should consist of a punchy list of the key elements that you have covered in the main body. For maximum impact, it is vital that you resist the urge to elaborate beyond a list of headings. Any description of what lies underneath the headings will make the audience feel that you are saying the presentation again. This would be a huge turn-off, just at the time that you want their attention the most.

This factual summary list, without comment, is designed to appeal to the logical side – the *right* brains of the audience. The close should be created with their *left* brains in mind. Putting it more bluntly, it should be designed to appeal to their *guts*.

The End Spike

Ideally, the End Spike should be as sharp and compelling as its opening colleague. The first and last words in a presentation are the most likely to be remembered, so it is your presentational duty to make them worth remembering.

An effective End Spike will probably have much less of a shock and awe character than a typical First Spike. This is because there has to be an element of rounding off the audience's thoughts, rather than blowing them open. You should not want the closer to be so striking that it makes new questions arise in their mind that you now have no opportunity to answer.

The End Spike may have an emotional aspect. Perhaps it will include a call to action – something that you want the audience to do as a result of what they have heard from you.

Let's say that I am a director who is coming to the end of presentation that I have made to the board. I have been urging them to agree to back a particular solution to the company's IT problems. I have included three key elements. As well as summarizing them, I want to include a specific call to action that contains a hint of the emotional commitment I feel for the project:

> *'I want us to buy this system because of the savings it will bring, because it will make the lives of our managers easier, but most of all because of the positive effect it will have on our customer relationships.*

If we don't make the purchase now, we will stay stuck in the 19th century, while all our competitors have moved well into the 21st.'

This is your last chance to make an impression as a leader, so you must fight against the natural tendency to end with a whimper. The following (typical weak) efforts are more like the last gasps of a dying man than striking endings:

'Well, I think that I've covered most of the important points. Any questions?'

'I've run out of time, so I hope I have included everything you wanted. Thanks for listening.'

These are not the words of someone who is inspiring an audience to travel to his desired Finishing Position. They are the words of someone who just couldn't be bothered.

Finishing with a summary *and* an End Spike is certainly neat and tidy. Perhaps a bit *too* neat and tidy. There is more than a hint of contrived pedantry about a summary. If your presentation is very short, you might not need one, as your key elements will be fresh in the audience's mind and any hint of repetition may turn them off and actually drive them further away from your desired Finishing Position.

Spiking all the way

Spikes can have an important role *throughout* the presentation, rather than merely being a device to start and finish the whole thing with. In Chapter 3, I mentioned that a long presentation is best thought of and created as several separate presentations, with a different Micro-Statement at the core of each.

Each of those sub-presentations needs a Spike at the beginning and the end.

The Spikes within the main body will provide a sequence of pleasing jolts for the audience, thus maximizing the chance of you still winning the fight for their attention throughout the time you are in front of them.

Final Avoidance List

This is a dictatorial list of things *not* to do right at the end of the whole presentation:

1. Don't just stop dead at the end of a sentence that is clearly nor designed to be the *last* sentence. It will leave the audience feeling that they are hanging over the edge of a cliff.

2. Don't apologize for something that you have just realized that you have left out of the main body. You will probably be the only one who has noticed and closing with an apology is perhaps the weakest of all finishes.

3. Don't finish by asking a question. This would mean a massive loss of control, at a time when your control level should be at maximum. any way, it is your job to have answered all the questions during the time that you have been speaking.

4. Don't give an encyclopedic summary which effectively repeats the whole presentation.

5. Don't say 'Thank you'. An expression of gratitude is manifestly adequate, but it always sounds submissive. It is really another form of apology. 'Thank you' is a phrase used by someone who is too lazy to think of something else.

There will be many occasions during your presenting career when you will not have the time to write out every word of your presentation in advance. But even if you only have 10 minutes to prepare, use one of those minutes to write out your first sentence (your First Spike) *and* your last sentence (your End Spike).

This is the best way of moving your last words away from irrelevance towards immortality.

CHAPTER 7

NAIL IT ALL DOWN

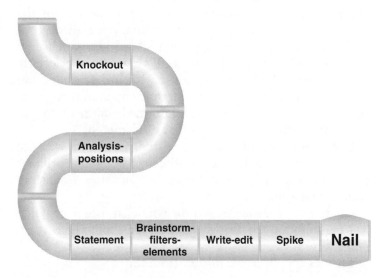

Knockout

Analysis-positions

Statement | Brainstorm-filters-elements | Write-edit | Spike | **Nail**

I f you are going to present effectively, preparing a Baseline Text is not enough. You have to nail it down in a form that is accessible under pressure. You need to find a way of ensuring that you are not struggling to find your words when you are fighting to keep the attention of the audience. This might involve using paper, cards or auto-cue. You may also involve a lectern or simply a table.

Whatever tools or techniques you choose, you must make an effort to ensure that you do justice to the words you have created. You have to feel that it would be a tragedy if you weren't able to get them from your brain to your lips.

Why Not Memory Alone?

In 2005, David Cameron almost managed to change the rules of Public Speaking. Even if you are a staunch Tory, I am absolutely certain that you cannot remember a single sentence of the speech that he made to the British Conservative Party conference in October of that year.

What you probably *can* remember is that he didn't use any notes and he stood centre-stage, well away from the lectern. He never took his eyes away from the audience.

On the other hand, his opponent, David Davis, delivered his speech from a typed-out script placed on the lectern. He was hesitant, clearly unfamiliar with his script and eye contact with the audience was intermittent, even though his content was considered by most informed commentators to be far more authoritative than that of Cameron.

But no-one in the audience cared. Cameron was the *persuader* and Davis merely the *reader*. One brilliant performance, one poor performance and the leadership contest was effectively over.

These two speeches altered the whole landscape of political presentation. In British politics, for about three years, notes were for wimps.

Business presenters can learn from this:

If you have a support staff of 20 people to help with the content of your speech....

If you have six months available to write it....

And if you can block out two weeks from your diary so that you can devote all that time to learning and rehearsing it....

Then you can forget about using a written-out script or notes.

But if you live in the real world, you cannot afford to rely on memory alone. Presentation is always a high-pressure activity. There is too much of a danger that you will forget to say something crucial. There is something about a crowd of faces staring at you which seems to partially paralyze the relevant part of the brain.

And think of the feelings of the audience. That distinctive look on the face of a speaker who has suddenly realized that he just cannot remember what to say is one of the great horrors that we would all like to avoid looking at. Even if we don't like the speaker as a person, his suffering is quickly transferred to us and our bladders.

Another disadvantage of relying on memory alone is that it can also look as though you're winging it. The obvious existence of some form of notes makes it clear that you have had the courtesy to prepare something for this audience instead of just blagging with stuff that you are making up as you go along.

So ... you need a reliable *delivery reminder system*. The three systems that I recommend you consider are notes on cards, full script on paper or full script on auto-cue.

A fully written-out script would guarantee that you do not leave anything out. It might also be the cause of a stilted, wooden delivery. Ironically, David Cameron is now afflicted with this problem. He has come to realize that even someone with his spectacular memory cannot learn 70 minutes of material, much of which has been created or re-written within the previous 24 hours. Between 2007 and March 2010, he delivered all his most important speeches from a full script that has been placed in front of him on a lectern.

Freewheeling, wandering Dave, the public speaker who lived on the edge, seemed to have gone for good. However, he went back to using no notes for his speech to the 2010 Conservative Party Spring Conference. This was a clearly a decision that was meant to make him look as impressive a leader as possible.

During the rest of the election campaign, Cameron continually showed that he has an incredible memory under pressure. This culminated in a remarkable speech in front of 10 Downing Street, just before he entered it for the first time as Prime Minister. In the space of four minutes, he managed to include gracious words about his predecessor, a detailed policy agenda, an emotional disclosure of his personal beliefs and an echo of John F Kennedy.....*all without a note in sight.*

Please remember that David Cameron is perhaps the best political presenter in the world (with no Obama-style auto-cue addiction). He is superb, but not a realistic role model.

I urge you to only impose on yourself a regime of continuous high-pressure no-notes presentation the next time that you are running for Prime Minister.

By the way, I do accept that my colleagues in the professional speaking fraternity can speak for hours without any form of prompt. But do remember that they are usually performing a set-piece that has not varied for months (or even years).

There *are* situations where a verbatim script could be the best option, including:

- award ceremonies with tight schedules;
- shareholders' meetings where every word has to be correct;
- major set-pieces in front of large audiences.

All the above scenarios will probably involve a production team. Cues for audio-visual support must be delivered precisely. The presenter cannot be allowed the freedom to speak off-piste.

Even if you are the chief executive of a multi-national (and I sincerely hope you are), it will only be on relatively few occasions that you will have to use a fully written-out script. Brief notes are the best weapon in the vast majority of business presentations, but tips on how to deliver from verbatim scripts, both from paper and auto-cue are given later in this chapter.

Notes

Carefully created notes can become your best friend, because they allow you to focus on what you are actually *saying*, rather than using up mental energy on desperately trying to remember what you need to say *next*.

I recommend that you use lined index cards. I have found that the best size is six inches by four inches. They are small enough to hold comfortably and large enough to hold a significant amount of information.

The only way to get a presentation right is to work continuously on it. Your ability to deliver a presentation effectively is as much about your knowledge of the cards as it is about knowledge of the whole Baseline Text.

You must therefore get your cards totally sorted out before rehearsal starts. Notes must be neat and calculated and clear enough so that they are your best friend when the pressure is on.

Carefully conceived notes ensure that the structure and content of the presentation is clear to you at all times. They eliminate the possibility that you will suddenly go blank: something that the audience dreads just as much as you do.

There is an additional benefit which is not immediately obvious. When I coach experienced corporate presenters, I sometimes encounter resistance when I bring up the topic of notes. It seems that some people regard notes as a sign of lack of virility:

> 'I have spent 20 years in this industry. I know all there is to know about Fund Management/Accountancy/ Potatoes. I know my stuff so well that I just don't need notes to remind me what to say.'

The problem is that *the presenter may actually know too much*. We have already emphasized the importance of editing. Editing is the process that stops the presentation becoming a Brain Dump of everything that the presenter knows about the subject: the content is pruned–until it just consists of the information that the audience really needs to know.

The enormous value of editing is lost if the presenter does not have an immediately accessible link to the Baseline Text in front of him, i.e. notes. If you merely rely on their memory, it is highly likely that you will include material that has been deliberately and ruthlessly eliminated during the final stages of preparation. The impact of editing will be lost.

The best way of developing notes is to go through a specific process:

- Read the Baseline Text out loud.
- Divide it into digestible chunks that reflect changes of topic and potential change of pace.
- Re-read each chunk separately and highlight the words that are distinctive enough to remind you of a sentence or sequence of sentences.
- Copy the distinctive words onto a card in block capitals.
- Now see if you can remember and say out loud the passage from the text, just using the card as a memory prompt.
- As you carry on practicing, continue to delete words until such time as you are able to recall the material using the smallest possible number of words, checking back to the Baseline Text for accuracy.

Here is an example of notes being created from a full script:

'Selling Protection products is the triumph of common-sense over wishful thinking.

Car companies rave about it: ABS, safety glass and airbags.

Security Suppliers recommend alarms, locks and light sensors.

High Street chemists have a one- size-fits-all solution in a variety of colours, flavours and textures.

What I am talking about is Protection.'

It might finally end up on a card like this ...

> **TRIUMPH**
> **CAR RAVE – BAGS**
> **SECURITY – SENSORS**
> **CHEMIST – COLOURS**

The creation of a noted card like this is a highly personal process. The words I have chosen to put on the card are the ones that I believe would remind *me* of the words in that paragraph of the Baseline Text. These particular words may not work for you. You might need more ... or less.

The first time you try this, you will find that you need a relatively large number of words to remind you of a relatively small part of the Baseline Text. Don't be frustrated by this. This is a skill that evolves over a period of time.

I recommend that it is one you develop on your own now, rather than trying to climb up the learning curve the day before your next presentation. The best way of doing this is to randomly choose a paragraph from a published speech (you can find thousands of the internet). Or you can use any corporate document or even a novel. Then try to boil down the paragraph onto a card as above and, just using the card to remind you of the text, try to say the text out loud as precisely as possible.

Experiment with different words and different arrangements of words. You will soon find that you are able to convey over 80% of the words from the original, perhaps using one striking word to remind you of several sentences.

I have deliberately made the exercise above as hard as possible ... by suggesting that you hone your noting down techniques on words originally conceived by someone else. It will be much easier do when you have lovingly and painfully created the words.

When you go through the sequence above with your own material, don't fall in love with the first set of notes you create. In fact, you should assume that your first notes will definitely not be the ones you will eventually use in anger. Your final notes should only come into existence as you become more and more familiar with your presentation. If you rehearse out loud several times, you will find that you can gradually reduce the number of words on each card, and probably also the number of cards.

This is a highly desirable result for two reasons:

1. The fewer notes you have, the less time you will spend looking down and the more time you will spend in eye contact with the audience.

2. The fewer cards you have, the more control you are likely to have over them in your hands. You certainly don't want to be constantly shuffling a thick pack as though you were itching to go to Las Vegas.

A small number of cards means that you are less likely to lose your place under pressure, whether they are in your hands, on a table or on a lectern.

Total Familiarity

Eventually, you will get comfortable with your final set of cards … the ones you will rely on in front of the actual audience on the day. You should consider adding some directions to yourself in a different colour to the script words on the card, such as, MOVE CENTRE STAGE or SLOW DOWN. Asterisks can act as reminders for when to change slides need to be changed.

Your final set of cards should be:

- neat and tidy, with no crossings-out;
- written in block capitals (it's amazing how unfamiliar your own handwriting can look when people are staring at you);
- clearly numbered, just in case you drop them;
- mainly single reminder words, with the occasional longer phrase;
- widely spaced.

If they have all the above characteristics, they can become your closest ally in your fight to keep the audience's attention. You should aim to become totally familiar with them, so that you can picture them in your mind's eye, almost without looking at them. This ensures that every time you glance down at them on the day, you get a warm glow of recognition. This should be a key confidence builder for you.

Using Cards Under Pressure

They can be placed on a table or lectern in front of you, or held at waist level in one hand. You should try to get comfortable with them whether there is any form of structure in front of you, or whether there is nothing to protect you from the hungry audience.

Try to avoid holding them in both hands: you will look like a priest who is trying to create his own pulpit.

However, your overall aim is *not* word-for-word perfection: your aim should be for you to get the essence of the meaning across. This does *not* mean that you shouldn't have bothered to go through the pain of deciding on the exact words of your script in advance. However, it *does* mean that you should not feel that those words are a straightjacket.

The rhythm that you need to get used is as follows:

- Absorb
- Lift
- Speak

This means that you should be able to glance down at your card, immediately *absorb* a word or words that remind you of a sentence or two, and then *lift* your eyes up to look at the audience. Only then should you *speak*. This sequence takes a bit of getting used to … so practice hard at it.

At the time of writing, I have been a professional speaker for 22 years and I am proud to say that I always use cards every time I present. This is the case whether I am doing a speech that I have just written or one that I have done (with some adjustments) many times before.

I perform my keynote speech, *Fighting Talk*, to corporate audiences all over the world. It usually lasts for about an hour. Of course, I know my material extremely well. But my card is a very solid mental anchor for me. It allows me to adapt to how the audience are reacting to my words. I can improvise with new material that responds to an audience comment, and no matter how long this unscripted excursion lasts, I know that I can get back onto my pre-planned track just by glancing down at my card, which I usually place on a lectern or table within easy reach of wherever I am on the stage.

I have had to deal with a huge variety of interruptions to my train of thought, including fire alarms, microphones breaking down, sets crashing down behind me and audience members fainting (not usually as a reaction to the quality of my material).

No matter how long or intense the unexpected interruption, and no matter what I have had to say to deal with it, I have always been able to glance at my card and remember exactly where I was in the presentation and get back on track.

This ability has proved even more useful in front of rowdy After Dinner audiences. In this context, I will usually have my note card on the table in front of me. The audience is probably not even aware of its existence.

The card allows me to respond assertively to that most intense of audience-reactions: heckling.

A few years ago, I had the pleasure of addressing the *Liverpool Echo* Sportsman's Dinner. The black tie audience consisted of 300 scousers, who had already formed a preliminary view of me when the MC's introduction of me included the words, '... and so please welcome our guest speaker ... a barrister all the way from *London* ...'

I had managed to say the first three words of my speech when one of the guests, the comedian Stan Boardman, decided to shout out, 'You poor sod!' This caused a huge burst of laughter. Fortunately, I had come prepared for battle. I smiled and said, 'Sorry Stan, when I do a ventriloquist's act, I bring my own dummy.' The applause was rapturous. They were delighted that the soft southerner could fight back.

But this was only the opening skirmish. Stan was not going to be beaten off that easily. So he came back with another comment, again getting a big laugh. I then said, 'Stan has clearly never learned how to swim … because he has never been able to keep his mouth shut for long enough.'

The audience were baying for more by now. And so, someone else decided to have a go: the notorious local politician, Derek Hatton. His heckle didn't get a great response, so I was able to say, 'Derek, you don't understand … the idea of heckling is to make *me* look a prat.'

This Battle of Shining Wit went on for 10 minutes. Eventually, Stan said, 'Sod it, Graham … you win!'

He and Derek then raised their napkins over their heads in a sign of surrender. And I got a standing ovation even though I had hardly started my speech.

I can now reveal that I had an unfair advantage. As well as the card which had notes relating to my speech, I also had a card in front of me which had 30 heckler put-down lines taken from my database of jokes. Every time Derek and Stan shouted out, all I had to do was glance down to be reminded of another, apparently spontaneous missile.

The left side of the card looked like this:

> **DUMMY**
> **SWIM**
> **ME PRAT**
> **CLIP ON**
> **IQ**
> **FIRST GLASS**

If you want to find out what lines the last five words stand for, try heckling me next time you are in one of my audiences.

Paper Scripts

You should only choose the option of using a fully written-out paper script as your delivery mechanism if it is absolutely unavoidable. For instance, you may be a politician or a senior executive who has had the speech written for him by someone else. You may not have the time to make yourself familiar enough with the script so that you can reduce it to notes on cards ... and there is no auto-cue.

I urge you not to allow this to happen: it is always dangerous to use words that you do not own. Even if you are one of the tiny number of high-status individuals who use speechwriters all the time, I urge you to be as involved in the writing process as your frantic timetable allows.

However much or little you have written yourself, there are certain things that you must take control of:

1. Make the script deliverable

The script should be typed out, double-spaced, no smaller than 14-point, with every new sentence starting on a new line. Embolden words that you feel need particular emphasis. Most presenters find that Arial is the easiest type-face to read under pressure.

2. Get familiar with the script

Read the words carefully on paper at least three times, mouthing the words to yourself. Make certain that it contains no surprises and no unpronounceable words that may have slipped through the editing net ... .even if you have written every word yourself.

3. Ensure that there is a lectern

You will not be able to use a paper-based script if you have to hold it in your hands while delivering it. A speaker holding a sheaf of papers looks (and feels) hopelessly amateurish. Any nervous hand-shaking is unpleasantly exaggerated, and moving a used sheet to the bottom of the pile is a labour-intensive process that is very difficult to carry out with speed and comfort while an audience is watching you. A lectern saves you from this horror.

4.   Get used to the lectern

Place your script in a neat pile and then firmly fold over the top-left corner of the whole pile. This will make it easier to pick up each individual sheet during delivery. If the lectern is big enough, place the first sheet of the script on the left side and the rest of the script on the right. This allows you to use the first two sheets of the script before you have to move any paper while speaking. During rehearsal, practice picking up the 'used' sheet on the right of the lectern and transferring it swiftly to the left. Simply slide the paper across: there is no need to turn it over.

5.   Observe the 80/20 rule

You must not allow the performance of the speech to become a reading-out-loud exercise. Whenever you look down at the script, your level of familiarity with the words should be so high that each glance is merely a reminder of words that you already know. Look at the script 20% of the time and at the audience 80% of the time. Aim to increase the amount of audience eye-contact with each successive rehearsal.

6.   Suck and Spew

The above heading may be unpleasant, but it ensures that you will not forget the following technique. It is a way of minimizing the amount of time that you spend speaking while you are looking down at your notes. Essentially, you need to distinguish between the activities of reading and speaking. For any given sentence on paper, you should glance at it to absorb the words (*suck up*) and then look up at the audience before you actually say the words (*spew out*). During rehearsal, ask a trusted colleague to give you feedback on how effectively you are sucking and spewing.

Auto-Cue

Prompting systems are best suited to television professionals who have a large volume of words to present under high pressure in a precisely calculated time-slot. They are also the ultimate safety mechanism for politicians, especially in the USA. Ronald Reagan was the first one to use them properly. He was so good that, even when the media deliberately drew a lot of attention to what he was doing, his audiences still felt that his words were coming from his guts and not a piece of glass.

You may be in a situation where the speech has only just been written and/or it is vital that you don't get any of the words wrong. If a corporate event is big enough and important enough, with a budget to match, auto-cue can become your ultimate communication comfort blanket.

Getting the Script Ready

This is not just a case of just dumping the script you have on to the auto cue machine. It must be spaced and highlighted in such a way that it easy to read under pressure. This is best done with the person who will be operating the auto-cue machine for you on the day. They will also help you to select the font that works best for you.

Each new sentence should start on a new line. Words that require emphasis in delivery should be **emboldened,** while words that need extreme emphasis should be **<u>underlined</u>** as well. You might also include directions (such as the playing of videos) in bracketed (BLOCK CAPITALS).

Prior to your rehearsal with the prompting equipment, you must:

- have read the script on paper several times;

- have marked in where you would like the pauses and the breaks;
- have identified any words that you feel are particularly difficult to pronounce;
- have total control and familiarity with the script. There must be no words that are strangers to you.

Using the equipment to deliver

There are three main types of auto-cue: glass screen, plasma screen and floor monitor. But they all involve a vital human element as well: your relationship with the auto-cue operator. The operator needs to get used to the speed that you deliver and you need to learn to trust him. This means that you have to practice. This is the sort of technology where your level of comfort will increase hugely with each successive performance, and many presenters can achieve a high skill level very quickly indeed.

In fact, auto-cue is so easy to get used to that it becomes dangerously habit-forming for some presenters. Make sure that it only becomes something you like to use rather than something you *must* use.

Glass Screen

This is the most commonly available type. Two panes of glass stuck are placed at an angle on metal sticks with adjustable heights. They reflect the words of the script which is playing on a television screen below.

Theses two screens are normally placed in front of the speaker, about six feet apart. This allows you to look to the right and the left and thus maintain eye contact as well as script contact.

But remember that auto-cue should be used as a form of prompt and *not* merely a reading device. Use of the system should not involve a fixed stare at the words with just an occasional look at the audience. Good use of prompting consists of the presenter's eyes looking at the script 20% of the time and looking at the audience 80% of the time. Your mindset should be that you are not actually *reading*. You are *reminding* yourself of words that you already know.

When you rehearse with screens for the first time, be just a little playful. Experiment with using the left screen and then the right screen. Make sure that you are also spending as much time as you dare saying the words you have been reminded of while looking directly at the audience in the gap between the screens. Get used to pausing so that you become confident of the operator's ability to pause with you.

After rehearsing several times, you should feel that the glass screens are something that you are referring to, rather than something you are tied to.

Barack Obama has taken the use of split-screen auto-cue to new heights. Instead of the normal eight feet, he has the screens placed at least 16 feet apart, so that both his live audience and his television audience are almost unaware of their existence. He has the knack of sweeping a chunk of words off one of the screens and delivering them into everyone's faces as though they are coming straight from his heart and not from a machine. He never reads. He reaches out with his eyes.

However, he is also a case study in the dangers of auto-cue brilliance: he has become so good at using it that he *relies* on it. When he is forced by circumstance to speak with a paper script, notes or no notes, he is markedly less impressive.

Plasma Screens

These are devices that are usually placed on the wall behind the audience. Of course, this limits the size of audience and auditorium in which they can be used. Mind you, the audience shouldn't be too *small* either (i.e. less than 100 or so), because some of them will have an unstoppable urge to look behind them and read your words before you do!

The key advantage of using them is you don't have to stand behind a lectern. There is no physical barrier between you and the audience and you are free to move around on stage if you want to.

Using them still requires practice, but will be well worth it when you can feel the extremely high level of eye contact that you can achieve. The comfort and freedom you get from plasma screens is as exhilarating to the experienced presenter as downhill skiing with no clothes on. Apparently.

Floor Monitors

These are placed on the front of the stage or on the ground just in front of the stage. There would usually be three: left, right and centre. They are only a credible option if the stage is relatively high ... otherwise there is the danger that you will look down too much and the audience will spend most of their time looking at your forehead ... and if the presenter is me, being blinded by the glare.

But they are less expensive than plasma screens and can be credible even in front of audiences of 100 or less.

Even more than when you use the other two types of auto-cue, you must rid yourself of any feeling that you can use floor monitors as a reading device: sucking and spewing has to become second nature.

Rubberknecking

You have now almost got to the end of this chapter and I have yet to mention the most common delivery reminder system ... *because you shouldn't use it.*

Rubbernecking is my term for the common presentational practice of constantly turning round and reading from a sequence of bullet points from a screen behind you. Essentially, you would be using the slides as notes for yourself instead of as a visual aid for the audience. This becomes a grimly tedious experience for the audience as they look at a combination of your slides and your shoulder blades.

Unless you don't mind being boring, *just don't do it.*

In the next chapter, I will discuss this issue at greater length, but with far less restraint.

Chapter 8

SHOW IT ... IF YOU REALLY MUST

'Ask not what your slides can do for you. Ask what your slides can do for your audience.'

This is what John F Kennedy would have said if he had moved from politics into presentation coaching. The best visual aid is you, the presenter. You should avoid any tool that gets in the way of you effectively fighting for the audience's attention. You must be the main medium whether you are speaking to one person or 1000.

In the corporate arena, it often seems that far more energy is directed towards producing slides than creating persuasive words. More effort is made to get into the memory of the laptop than into the mind of the audience. This results in an unfocused splurge of facts and figures; with the slides flickering across the screen fast enough to induce epilepsy.

The visuals are thus used as an unspoken excuse for not properly selecting the words that have to be *said* in order to get the job done.

It is not just the sheer number of slides that is the problem: there is an urge to fill each slide to bursting point, with verbose text that seems to have been laid out by a sadistic optician. The real value of the content has been obscured by a bullet-point blizzard.

The Myth

This is the great corporate presentational myth:

'The slides are the presentation and spoken words are merely there to back up the slides.'

Despite my best efforts at independent intervention, business speakers continue indiscriminately to unleash the most destructive weapon of mass presentation: **PowerPoint**.

I use the word 'PowerPoint' to represent all makes of presentation software, in the same sweeping way that the word 'aspirin' is often used to describe all forms of pain relief tablets ... a remedy that is often sought by those who suffer an overdose of watching slide-infested presentations.

PowerPoint is the single biggest cause of boring presentations in the 21st century. It encourages you to create a sequence of slides which is not merely support for the presentation: it *is* the presentation. The packaging should come with this instruction:

'Engage Auto-Content Wizard and Disengage Brain.'

PowerPoint was designed as a tool to enhance the *delivery* of a presentation. But it has actually become the most commonly used tool for *content development*. In fact, the existence of an overly complex encyclopaedia of slides is regarded by many companies as proof of preparation. Instead of thinking about the necessary result and what he needs to say to achieve it, the PowerPoint Black Belt dives straight into slide creation, while forgetting something vital:

PowerPoint is *not* the presentation. What *you* actually *say* is the presentation. PowerPoint should only be there as *support*.

Enthusiasm for the subject rather than the technology is a vital ingredient for every Bare Knuckle Presenter. Only an enthusiastic speaker can make other people enthusiastic. That is how presentations can make things happen. Remember that enthusiasm can be strangled by a combination of verbosity and visual overload: presentations that are too long and too detailed ... and with too many slides. And those slides are put up in a non-stop stream, defended with words like: 'Of course I am not reading the slides – they just remind me of the points that I need to cover.' (Translation: 'I haven't bothered to create a script or notes and I desperately need the slides to give me a vague idea of what to say next')

If you need notes, put them on cards, as described in Chapter 7. Cards never break down, hibernate or run out of battery.

PowerPoint can be thought of as a drug which should be prescribed sparingly, if at all. When misused, it has unpleasant side effects which include laziness, verbosity and pedantry. In fact, PowerPoint obsession is so strong in Britain and America that it is now no longer just software ... it has become a *god*. To criticise is to blaspheme. Here is the prevailing attitude:

> 'But we have to use PowerPoint. If we don't, no one will take us seriously. After all, we have always used it and all our competitors use it. Damn it, everyone expects us to use it. That's the way it's always been.'

The manual that comes with PowerPoint even says 'to create presentations, you write and design slides.' This perpetuates the myth that PowerPoint *is* the presentation. The presenter has become a laptop with a larynx.

I have never known anyone walk out of a conference and say:

> 'Wow, what a great conference. But it would have been even better if the presenters had used more PowerPoint. Mind you, I can remember all 43 slides from the finance director's presentation. And when I get back to my room I will thoroughly review this booklet containing the other 171 slides that were used during the course of the day ... because I have no life and no friends.'

The Reality

If you have managed to get this far without throwing the book away in disgust, then there is a chance that your mind is open enough to consider a more combative attitude:

Use PowerPoint as a weapon, not wallpaper.

The words that you actually *say* in the presentation are more important than the ones that the audience *read*. You are not just a presenter: you are also a *leader*.

To fulfil both roles simultaneously, you have to maintain control by keeping the audience's focus on you and on what you are saying. This should always be their *primary* focus.

Any visuals that you may use should only be their *secondary* focus. If the visuals claim the majority of their attention, you have effectively given up your position of leadership. You will also have given up your chance to really connect with them because you are subordinate to your slides.

Bare Knuckle Presenting is about the transfer of ideas and information between individuals. This human-to-human transfer can only occur if you, the presenter, really are the *centre* of attention.

You should also be wary of Audio-Visual Anaesthesia. A constant flow of slides can have a terminally numbing effect on an audience, especially just after lunch or late in the afternoon. The flickering screen can soothe them to sleep.

Equally dangerous is the effect it has on you, the presenter. Even if you are normally a dynamic and assertive performer, you will find that this aspect of your character is critically dulled by the presence of slides behind you.

Practical Use

Now that I have taken a breath from my ranting, it's time for me to surprise you with one of my core beliefs:

PowerPoint is fantastic … when it is used in a *miserly* fashion.

I have already said that PowerPoint is a presentational weapon. But it is a *specialized* weapon, which should not be used automatically in every situation.

This brings us, at last, to the Bare Knuckle core attitude to slides:

You must use the smallest number of slides that is compatible with getting the audience to the Finishing Position, without detracting from your own presentational pre-eminence.

In other words:

For maximum impact,

Have minimal slides

The question is not

'Do you need the slides?'

The question is

'Does your audience need the slides?'

You have probably had enough of me moaning. There are some rare occasions when the presentation dictator within me will graciously allow you to use a few slides, so it's time for me to give you a mental framework in which to do it.

Your Slide Mindset

If you have followed my advice so far, you will have written a Baseline Text with an appropriate Micro-Statement, Key Elements and Spikes. You feel confident that the presentation contains sufficient overlap between your own agenda and the needs of the audience. But you suspect that there is something missing ... or perhaps you are certain. There are certain concepts and pieces of information that you feel would be much easier to get across visually. You may well be right.

But this suspicion needs to be tested. Using the draft of the script, do a 'talk through' to yourself. Mark every point where you feel that a visual is *absolutely necessary* for an audience to appreciate what you are saying.

Sadly, I have lost count of the number of times I have been brought in at the last moment to coach presenters whose habit is to do the exact opposite. They obsessively create a massive slide pack and realize rather belatedly that the audience might like to hear a few words to go with them.

I have then had to ask the client to jilt their visuals so that they can travel through the Preparation Pipeline with me instead. This has often been a traumatic parting, even though they realize that they have been trapped in a bad relationship with their slideware.

As tablets of stone (one of the oldest types of visual aid) are so expensive these days, I only have five commandments for using slides if you really must:

The Bare Knuckle Slide Commandments

1. Only use them when they *emphatically* add impact to the spoken word.

2. Only use slides which can by instantly absorbed.

3. Choose to use pictures and graphics instead of text every time.

4. Avoid bullet-points (except for summaries, not speaker notes).

5. Avoid narratives (they are for paper, not screens).

Let's examine each piece of PowerPoint pontification:

1. Emphatic Impact

No matter how eloquent your choice of words, there are some things that just need to be shown. In the same way as exceptionally appropriate words can move an audience, so too can just the right image.

An incredibly cute puppy with a sorrowful expression will be more quickly and memorably assimilated via the audience's eyes than a mere description of one. A new product model is better seen than described. Some statistical information has far more impact in a visual format than a solely verbal one.

Your attitude should be that the burden of proof is on the slide. **Every single slide will have to fight its way into your presentation.** Only the highest-impact enhancer can make the cut.

The key skill here is to select a small number of really striking slides. This ensures that the audience really enjoys and appreciates each one. Too many, and the slides distract rather than stimulate.

Just because a slide has managed to get into your presentation, it doesn't have an automatic right to stay there. Don't ask how many you should have. *Ask yourself how many can you get rid of.*

The answer to the questions below will help:

'Does this slide show something to which I cannot do full justice by words alone?'

'Is this slide adding something that has not been covered on previous slides?'

'Does this slide make an impact when it appears for the first time?'

If the answer to each of the above questions is *Yes,* then that slide is a good candidate for inclusion.

Most slide remote controls now provide the option of going to a blank or black screen. This is a great innovation because it means that you are able ensure that your audience has no alternative to looking straight at you. Instead of, or in conjunction with this, you could use something like a logo slide that would not necessitate anything more than a passing glance from the audience while continuing to provide brand endorsement.

2. Instantly Absorbed

When it is completely necessary to use a slide I follow the advice of my esteemed colleague, Warren Evans (a self-confessed industrial strength PowerPoint user). All visuals need to be what he calls '*insta-absorb*'. This means the audience needs to be able to glance at a slide and instantly absorb what they are looking at.

Pictures, and *well done* graphs and charts have this characteristic. The only type of slide that has this characteristic is a slide that has no more than five lines of text, with no more than three words in a line. If you use any more than three words, the audience has to consciously read them.

Make them as bold and easy-to-see as a motorway road sign:

Paris 3 miles

Strasbourg 42 miles

Berlin 319 miles

In the same way a driver should not take their eyes off the road for a moment longer than necessary to see a road sign, so audiences should not take their eyes off *you* for any longer than is absolutely necessary.

Avoid long textual extracts, huge numeric tables and dense diagrams that are just dumped into a slide.

3. Pictures and Graphics beat Text

Some business concepts, especially financial ones, can be immediately and compellingly captured and conveyed by a graph, bar chart, flow chart, pie chart or similar. If the same information was written out as text, the presentation becomes a public reading contest in which the presenter finishes last.

A picture may be as good as a thousand words, but this doesn't mean that a slide should have a thousand words on it.

Any diagram should have the least amount of words on it that is compatible with it being easily explained by you.

4. Bullet-Points are only for Summaries

They will never increase the adrenalin level of your presentation.

Bullet-Points are boring.

Let's face it: I know your dirty secret. You often use bullet-point slides as a memory prompt, don't you? Well, just stop it. Don't show the audience your notes. Keep them to yourself on a few low-tech, can't-break-down, highly adaptable cards.

However, summary slides are an effective way of drawing together your ideas and information. It could be an internal summary that allows one key idea in your presentation to be closed off. Alternatively, it could function as the end-of-presentation summary that *encapsulates* the whole proposition prior to the End Spike.

Bullet point text must be cut down to the bare minimum... just the key words or even a single word from the concept you are presenting. You should certainly not use full sentences.

Using a slide as a summary is a device that is welcomed by audiences who have sat through any presentation that is long enough to tax their memory. Give them a heading plus one- or two-word bullet-points that concisely capture the Key Elements of your presentation:

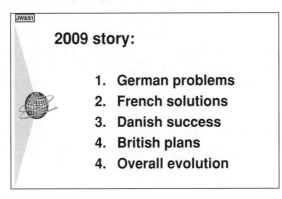

123

I will now be a little more proscriptively draconian:

Never put more than five bullet-points on a slide, and never have more than three words per point.

For instance, have a look back at my Five Bare Knuckle Slide Commandments. This is the summary slide you might use to capture them:

> **Five Commandments**
>
> 1. Add impact
> 2. Instant absorb
> 3. Every time
> 4. Summaries not notes
> 5. Paper not screen

Their slightly cryptic nature is intentional. These bullet points should not make sense on their own. They must only come to life when you breathe it into them through your vocal chords. This ensures that it is your spoken word that is the crucial communication factor. The slide is not leading the audience, *you* are.

5. Narratives are for Paper Documents

When you feel that there may well be a significant amount of possibly relevant information that you cannot fit into your spoken presentation, you should consider whether a narrative back-up document should also be made available to the audience. The document should be a narrative, i.e. fully grammatical sentences (unfashionable though that concept may be to anyone who left secondary education after 1990). It is something that you should actually want them to read, rather than glance at casually.

Unless you are utterly bound by house rules in your organization or industry, I urge you to make this a leave-behind rather than a sent-in-advance or given-out-at-the-start document. If an audience member reads it days, hours or even minutes before you speak, there is a real danger that they will have already made up their mind on the issue.

Essentially, you run the risk that human interaction, the live element of your presentation, will not be the dominant persuasive force. The document potentially becomes a dead weight that will crush the life out of your presentation before it has even started.

I also urge you not to give them a document them just as you start to speak, because the written word will inevitably compete against your voice for their attention. They cannot focus both on what they are reading and on you at the same time.

If you really must...

I know that you will still be tempted to create textual slides (other than summary slides), even though I have forbidden you from using them. What follows will show you how to do it if you desperately want to. (For more detail, the best source is www.thinkoutsidetheslide.com, and the book by Dave Paradi you can order there). So please walk with me into another pipeline (kindly provided by Warren Evans).

The PowerPoint Pipeline

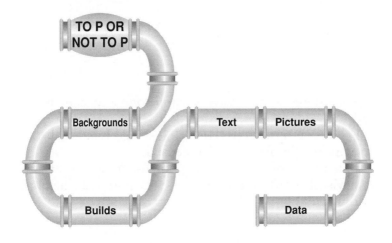

I won't labour this stage again. I hope you have gone through a lot of constructive and character-building pain before finally deciding to use slides. Now it's time to show you how to actually create them.

One of the ways to just about guarantee that your slide show will be grim is to give the task to a PA who has been on a basic slideware training course.

Your slides will look like everyone else's: too busy, too many, and with a brutally boring metronome of predictability.

Here's a default slide master from one software program:

Click to edit Master title style

Click to edit Master text styles
Second level
Third level
Fourth level
Fifth level

This thing is too busy even before any content is added.

When you open PowerPoint, you should remove all the defaults like this from your master slide.

This is one of a few basics *you* must master to ensure your visuals don't end up hurting you more than helping you.

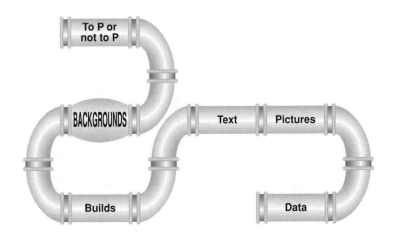

Backgrounds

Every software program will let you view master slides. This is the part of the program that sets the background that will appear on all your slides.

Use it. But don't over-use it.

Resist the temptation (and the defaults) of adding in your logo, corporate information, title of the presentation, date and time, etc on to every slide. It's busy and boring.

In the same way, beautiful graphic renditions with swirls, multiple colours and gradations, and artistically composed layers are not only unnecessary but often counter-productive.

Your backgrounds should allow strong contrasts. Graduated colour makes things a little more interesting than if it were just a solid colour. Blue is a safe bet, but green is a disaster.

You can add one piece of graphic. A logo or bar on one side or other bit of visual that prevents a totally blank background. This is an *insert*, or *paste*, exercise as you would use in any other piece of software.

Now you're ready to add the bits of text, pictures, or charts that have won the fight of persuading you then can enhance your presentation.

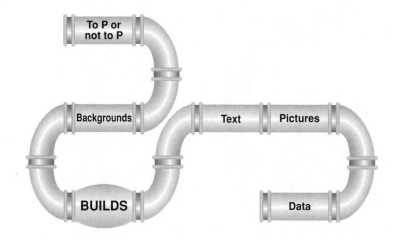

Builds

Talking about builds at this point in your PowerPoint Pipeline may seem a bit counter-intuitive. After all, wouldn't animating your slides be something you do after you've created the slides?

But it is vital that you are always thinking about how your slides exactly integrate with what you are saying.

First: avoid all exotica. You are not Stephen Spielberg, and this is not a special effects show. In any software you can make your text and graphics zoom, fly, spin, and do all sorts of things that may seem 'cool'. Cool, but distracting. In PowerPoint, just because you *can* do something does not mean you *should* do it.

The reason to use builds is simply to make sure that your audience stays with you, thus avoiding the tedious unpleasantness of reading point 5 while you are still dealing with point 1.

You also need builds to make items on the screen go away when you are done with them, leaving only your background showing, so that the audience focuses back onto you.

When you are delivering the presentation, you can encourage the audience's attention on to the screen by turning to face it for a moment. Even though your visuals will be insta-absorb, you should think of 'insta' as meaning a couple of seconds.

Never put something on the screen and then keep talking while they are absorbing it.

This is because:

1. They can either absorb the screen or listen to you, not do both at the same time.

2. Trying to do both subconsciously irritates them.

The overall effect is that they have not absorbed your screen material, they have not heard what you just said, and they are mad at you as well. This triple hit is part of what makes badly done PowerPoint so deadly to sit through.

Only have two build formats and both should be:

Fast: When it is time for the audience to see this item, then let them see it all immediately. No one wants to watch words appear one letter at a time, or pictures filled in like jigsaw pieces appearing one by one.

Focused: Words should appear in the exact position that you want them to be when the audience reads them. Don't make them dance in from a far corner of the screen.

Natural: Part of making things insta-absorb is delivering it the way that people are most naturally inclined to receiving it. We read from left to right. Text should appear that way if you choose a linear build.

Slide Creation Sequence
Create one text box, and completely detail it as to position on the screen, all its build functions, text size and colour.

Then copy and paste that text box everywhere else you will using a similar text. Now you have achieved consistency throughout your presentation in one shot.

All you need to do is change the letters inside each text box.

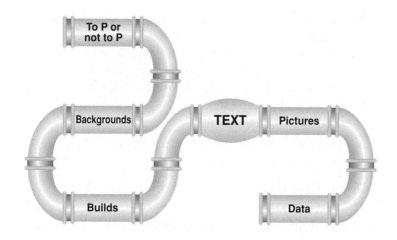

Creating Text

Open a text box, and put your first bit of text in it. (that 'bit' being two or three words)

Next pick a font. Sans serif (Arial; Helvetica) is actually easier to read on screen that serif (Courier; Times Roman).

No text on any presentation slide should ever be less than 36 point type in size, and always bold faced.

Skip the shadow boxes, back fills, contrast lines, etc, and ignore the 'art' options for words.

Now pick a colour. Pick one that contrasts with your background.

Yellow against a dark is very good, with white on a dark close behind, but red is always hard to read.

Keep in mind that the rich colours and crisp rendition of your computer screen will not be replicated when the image is blown up to many multiples of this size and projected on a screen. The reason so many presenters who should know better end up with unreadable slides is because they look fine on their PA's monitor, and the PA never sees them in an auditorium.

Then animate it as described above.

Then position it where you want it. Now you are ready to copy and paste, as described.

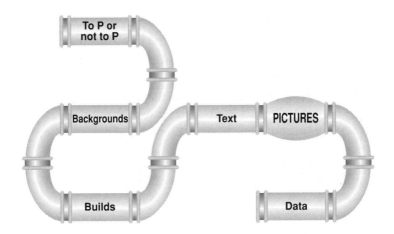

Pictures

We've already talked about animating pictures. I use 'pictures' to mean any graphic image you might use.

There are a myriad of places to get royalty-free pictures on the web these days.

Do **not** use any picture or image without complying with the usage agreement of its owner. Pictures are intellectual material. Copying and pasting them without permission is theft. This very specifically also applies to cartoons.

Do get your pictures into jpeg format. They take less space, and make it easier for your software to handle.

Size of Picture?

Here are three key thoughts:

1. Make it as large as you can, without covering up your border graphic (very distracting) or impinging on the bottom third of the screen.

2. Make it as large as you can while maintaining an acceptable resolution.

   If you stretch it too much, it will start to get fuzzy, and it will always look fuzzier on the screen that it does on your monitor.

3. Show only the part you want. Learn to use your crop function so that you can trim the sides of a picture to leave only the core that is what is going to make an impact your audience.

If your image is just for a smaller part of the screen, bigger is still better. I can't insta-absorb something if I'm struggling to figure out what I'm looking at.

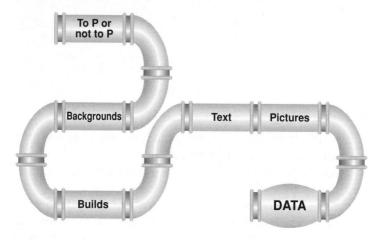

Data

If you are certain that a statistic, comparison, trend line, or other bit of hard information will have substantially more impact when presented visually, then it is worth a few extra minutes to do it properly.

Doing it properly does not abandon any of my Bare Knuckle principles. From your reservoir of information, ask yourself these questions:

- What is the bare minimum of information the audience *needs* to have to drive home your point?
- How do you create a visual of this that adheres to the insta-absorb commandment?

Presenters who don't ask these questions tragically subject their audiences to slides like this:

	A	B	C	D	E	F	G	H	I	J
6		national conference		2009				2010		
7			2009	Approved	2009	2010	2010	Approved	2010	2010
8		BUDGET STATEMENT	Projected	Budget	Actual	Budget	Projected	Budget	Actual	Budget
9			as of Dec 1	115 full	101 full	100 full	as of Dec 1	115 full	101 full	100 full
10		REVENUE								
11										
12		Full Registration	£49,313.00	£40,250.00	£36,329.00	£30,800.00	£49,313.00	########	£36,329.00	£30,800.00
13		Support Team	£4,865.00	£1,800.00	£1,840.00	£1,800.00	£4,865.00	£1,800.00	£1,840.00	£1,800.00
14		One Day Only	£2,400.00	£3,000.00	£3,400.00	£1,400.00	£2,400.00	£3,000.00	£3,400.00	£1,400.00
15		Meals	£910.00	£500.00	£888.00	£375.00	£910.00	£500.00	£888.00	£375.00
16		Sponsorship	£2,500.00	£5,000.00	£4,000.00	£6,000.00	£2,500.00	£5,000.00	£4,000.00	£6,000.00
17		Resource Table	£1,200.00	£1,200.00	£910.00	£1,000.00	£1,200.00	£1,200.00	£910.00	£1,000.00
18										
19		Total Revenue	£61,188.00	£51,750.00	£47,367.00	£41,375.00	£61,188.00	########	£47,367.00	£41,375.00
20										
21		EXPENSES								
22										
23		Promotion	£3,515.00	£5,000.00	£5,138.00	£5,700.00	£3,515.00	£5,000.00	£5,138.00	£5,700.00
24		Banquet	£1,886.00	£700.00	£1,903.00	£700.00	£1,886.00	£700.00	£1,903.00	£700.00
25		Speaker Liaison	£500.00	£675.00	£1,628.00	£675.00	£500.00	£675.00	£1,628.00	£675.00
26		Resource Table	£400.00	£800.00	£830.00	£800.00	£400.00	£800.00	£830.00	£800.00
27		Convention Chair	£1,235.00	£450.00	£518.00	£450.00	£1,235.00	£450.00	£518.00	£450.00
28		Sponsorship	£0.00	£500.00	£184.00	£500.00	£0.00	£500.00	£184.00	£500.00
29		Audio Visual	£640.00	£7,000.00	£1,695.00	£1,035.00	£640.00	£7,000.00	£1,695.00	£1,035.00
30		Facilities	£7,285.00	£2,500.00	£1,921.00	£2,020.00	£7,285.00	£2,500.00	£1,921.00	£2,020.00
31		Contingency	£5,000.00	£200.00	£1,155.00	£3,500.00	£5,000.00	£200.00	£1,155.00	£3,500.00
32		Total Meals (see below)	£26,248.00	£18,000.00	£14,675.00	£12,840.00	£26,248.00	########	£14,675.00	£12,840.00
33										
34										
35		Total Expenses	£46,709.00	£35,825.00	£29,647.00	£28,220.00	£46,709.00	########	£29,647.00	£28,220.00

When this was an available option:

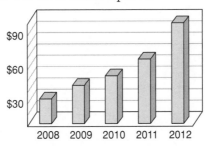

Remember that all good data graphics are purpose made, rather than thrown together from copy and paste. Everything that ends up on a slide should be hand crafted to perfectly support what is being said. And following the advice here, learning only what is necessary to do so, means that you can do it quickly.

A bespoke attitude to slides is just as necessary as a bespoke attitude to the words that you say.

If you adopt and use the principles in this chapter, you will have a very simple relationship with your slides: one of Master/Mistress and occasional servant. You will be in control of that relationship at all times.

Now it is time to shut your laptop and consider just what else you need to control.

Chapter 9

CONTROL YOURSELF

To be a Bare Knuckle Presenter, you do not have to be totally fearless. However, you do have to learn to *control* any fear that presenting may provoke.

Fear usually arises from situations where you are concerned that you might suffer some sort of harm because of lack of the necessary control. This chapter deals with control of both the internal (your state of mind) and the external (how you sound and look). You should definitely do as much as you can to control both.

Control your Nerves

If you suffer from nerves, you *will* present badly. You will shake, you will blush, and you will sweat. You will feel dizzy and forget your lines. Your audience will stare at you with a mixture of pity and contempt. They will hate you because you have made them feel even sicker than you do. No one is available to beam you back to the USS Enterprise.

For several years, everyone in that audience will remember 'The day you died'.

Now: *pause and rewind*. All the above can and has happened to experienced presenters ... but you can avoid it because you will be mentally prepared for battle.

There are good reasons to fear speaking. Audiences spot very quickly if you are:

- ill prepared;
- boring;
- patronizing;
- slide reading;
- wasting their time.

Wasting time is the 21st century's biggest corporate crime. If an audience feels that it is happening to them, you will see them react physically. Arms will fold. Eyes will go down to the table or up to the ceiling. Heads will shake, conversations will start and text messages will be sent.

You will be able to *smell* their resentment. You should also *fear* it ... and avoid causing it.

Never try to conquer this fear: instead you must *use* it. Use it to force yourself to prepare properly. The single biggest cause of bad presenting is failure to prepare.

It is obvious to an audience if a speaker has prepared well. They feel flattered, not just by the presentation itself, but by also by the effort made to prepare. You have paid them a compliment. You have made it clear that they are worth the effort.

Just imagine the opposite situation. Minimal preparation: no Audience Analysis, no focused Micro-Statement or sharp editing. You just get up and talk.

They will smell you instantly:

'Seems quite confident. Seems to know his subject. But what does he really want us to remember? Why doesn't he realize that most of what they are saying is not relevant? Wait a minute ... he's just winging this ... he hasn't actually prepared a word of it ... he just couldn't be bothered ... shows how important he thinks *we* are!'

Sometimes you will get away with it. But not often. You will look lazy and they will hate you for it.

If you do not fear audience hatred, please throw this book away now.

Use the fear as a cattle prod for preparation.

'Many people have the will to win.

Few people have the will to prepare to win'

Some American Bloke

The single biggest weapon in your armoury for combating nerves is the Bare Knuckle Pipeline. You will have used it to create a Micro-Statement driven Baseline Text that carefully caters for the needs of the audience and takes them where you want them to go. You should feel as confident as a chef who has cooked a superb dish and who is about to bring it to the table and serve it to the guests.

But imagine this: you have spent several days preparing what you know to be a good Baseline Text. You know that you have done as much preparation and rehearsal as you possibly can.

Unfortunately, you still feel sick.

It is the day of the presentation. You don't want to eat. You don't want to make eye contact, let alone speak to anyone. There is a constant lurch in the pit of your stomach. Your shoulders are stiff and your bowels are loose.

These symptoms can crush your presentation skills. You might not be able to get rid of the symptoms completely, but there is a lot you can do to fight them down to a manageable level.

Specific Techniques

Be proud of the preparation you have done

More than anything, this is what should give you the foundation of a nerveless performance. The audience may be disagree with significant parts of what you have prepared, but even the most hostile group is likely to respect the effort you have clearly out into the preparation.

Practice

If you have put in all the effort I have recommended, you will have created a superb Baseline Text and some very clear notes. You must not waste all this hard work by testing the material for the first time in front of the audience you actually need to persuade.

I have learned a lot from theatrically-minded conference producers who are used to the strict discipline of rehearsal. You should pay heed to their insistence that any presentation rehearsal process must be a true representation of what will happen on the actual day of performance.

I refer to this as *Battle Conditions Immersion.*

This is something you should build up to rather than imposing it on yourself as a sudden shock. Make sure that you are entirely familiar with your Baseline Text and chosen delivery mechanism (paper, cards or tele-prompt). Stand and say those words several times ... first of all on your own, and then in front of a trusted colleague or colleagues. Or even a Presentation Coach....if you can afford one.

Listen to the feedback you get, but be wary of altering very much of the actual content: this semi-private practicing should be focused mostly on delivery, not re-creation of material.

Next, if possible, step up the level of pre-bout intensity. If a presentation is important enough, you must rehearse it under the conditions you will be subjected to on the day. Anything else is just not a real rehearsal.

Every rehearsal must start from the moment before you get up to speak and there must be no asides or deviations from the presentation.

If you make a major mistake in rehearsal, press on without a 'sorry' or any other flag, unless you absolutely must stop, at which point you must go back to the beginning.

So ... get your rehearsal environment and your rehearsal *attitude* as close to the real thing as possible so you can go through all the same challenges exactly as you will on the day itself. Those challenges will include any nerves you might feel on the day. Every time you rehearse properly, those nerves will be reduced.

Re-channel

The symptoms of nerves are also the symptoms you had just before your first date (dry mouth, blushing, impotence). But the date was something you were looking forward to. This doesn't just happen to mere mortals. Professional golfers get this as they are walking up to the first tee, just like actors waiting backstage.

We are all boosted by adrenalin. This was the chemical that used to stimulate our ancestors when their lives were threatened. In the 21st century, it gives us a massive jolt when we are trying to cope with other crises.

But we are not *slaves* of adrenalin. It does not have to cause anxiety. You have to use it to give you a cutting edge. This is the key:

Change Anxiety to Anticipation.

Hmm … How trite. How easy to say in a book.

Well, try it. Visualize and Minimize.

Change vague fears into specific control, by analyzing them to death. Carefully list on a piece of paper exactly what things are feeding your anxiety. Make the list comprehensive, and elaborate further under each heading. You will find that the more you write about a particular fear, the less it stands up to scrutiny. By focusing this pedantically, you will make many of your anxiety sources dissolve before your very eyes.

The Tummy Clench

Despite your preparation and re-channelling you can still feel a black hole in your stomach. There is a temporary physical remedy: the tummy clench. Here is what you do:

- Sit upright.
- Put the fingers of one hand against your stomach.

- Think about the muscles just underneath your fingers.
- While breathing out, *clench* the muscles in your stomach that you would use to do a sit-up (if you can remember what one of those is) Do this hard enough so that it makes you lean forward slightly.
- Hold for three or four seconds.
- Relax.
- Repeat the process five times.

Gradually the sick feeling in your tummy will decrease. Apparently it is something to do with increasing the blood circulation to the area. I don't really care how it works. I just know that it *does* work.

The clench is actually quite hard work. If nothing else, it will certainly distract you from feeling pathetic.

First Word Focus

Just before the start of a race, athletes think of only one thing: their first step. They clear their minds of everything else. This is because they know that in a few moments, 100% of their being must be focused on that action.

In a similar way, just before you present, you have to eliminate irrelevant thoughts. You must focus all your energy on repeating to yourself the first sentence of your presentation. I don't mean out loud (you will look like Dustin Hoffman in *Rain Man*). The first words are your first step. Get them right and the preparation then has the chance to pay off.

Use the five techniques above in sequence, every time you present. Some will work for you and some won't. Nevertheless, the more often you present in a prepared and professional way, the less that nerves will be an issue for you. The day will come when you actually look forward to the prospect of presenting. You will get a sharp thrill from the off-piste feeling that you are about to do something brilliantly that most people would not want to do at all.

Control Your Voice

Your voice is a presentational weapon that you use very effectively every day. I will not ask you to tinker with it. I feel that breathing and voice control exercises are a waste of time. They are very boring and you will never get round to doing them.

All I want to do in this section is make you more aware of your voice ... and how you can change it just slightly to adapt to the challenges of presenting under pressure.

The Conventional View

Most presentation books will tell you that you should aim to speak in what they call a conversational tone that allows you just to be yourself. Well, that's not quite good enough, although it is a reasonable stance.

I certainly agree that you should never put on an act when you are presenting. Twenty-first century audiences are very quick to spot a fake persona. You need to make sure that there is no disconnect between the person that has walked into the room and the person that starts to present. Here is some feedback that should horrify you if you get it:

> 'You know, you were a completely different person when you were doing the actual presentation. I hardly recognized you!'

There is an understandable tendency to act un-naturally ... because formal presenting feels like such an un-natural activity compared to casual conversation. This is why:

In casual conversation, everyone gets a chance to speak. When you are presenting, only YOU get a chance to speak.

Of course, there will be small-audience situations where audience members will be talking back to you. But nearly all presenting involves an individual or a group entering into a tacit agreement that they will stay quiet and look at you for a significant period of time while you exercise a monopoly on the spoken word.

If you did this sort of thing in a pub, you would be considered a bore. But in a presentation, you must actively relish the opportunity to seize power.

An effective presentation is a one-way autocracy. The presentation should encourage thought, not dialogue. The presenter should want the audience to feel that they need to hear more from *them*, rather than needing to say something themselves.

This is why a conversational tone simply isn't good enough. A Bare Knuckle Presenter is not just a participant in a conversation: you must be far more striking than that. The audience should feel compelled to listen by the sharpness of your content and the intensity of your delivery.

I thought very carefully about the choice of the word *'intensity'* in the previous paragraph. I deliberately avoided 'passion'. This conjures up pictures of red faces and clenched fists hammering on tables. 'Enthusiasm' was also a candidate. But although enthusiasm is admirable in a sales director rallying the troops, it sounds weird when the finance director is explaining the need for 300 redundancies.

'Passion' and 'enthusiasm' sometimes strike a jarring note. Intensity never does.

Intense delivery is very difficult to describe on paper. But you know it when you hear it.

Intensity is something that connects with the audience on an emotional as well as an intellectual level. This formula captures what I am talking about:

Intellect plus Emotion LEADS TO➤ **appropriate intensity** LEADS TO➤ **audience engagement.**

Intensity is that ingredient which means that the audience feels it has no choice other than to listen. It makes them feel that any interruption would be rude. Most of all, it makes them feel that the presenter knows that he is worth listening to.

Capturing the Intensity

There is a way of 'picturing' the ideal level of intensity. Imagine you are a guest at a dinner party of about 12 people.

That should be easy. Now imagine that you are an invest-ment banker. That may not be easy ... but bear with me. You have spent 20 years advising small companies, arrang-ing finance for them and helping them through all sorts of difficulties. You are quietly proud of what you have done to encourage British business and make the country more prosperous.

But now comes the challenge. The host of the party is feeling mischievous. She gestures to the chap sitting next to her and says, 'John was just telling me that he thinks all investment bankers are over-paid parasites that are drag-ging our country down. Would you like to comment?'

Of course, she says this with a smile ... and there are a couple of chuckles around the table. But there is no doubt that a gauntlet has been thrown down.

Everyone turns to you, eagerly waiting your response.

The level of intensity that you would put into that response is the level of intensity that works for the vast majority of presenting situations.

You would try to come across as

- energetic, not angry;
- prodded, not provoked;
- challenged, not churlish.

What does it sound like?

We shall now try to pin down the precise characteristics of dinner-party intensity. It usually includes:

Your voice at a higher volume than in casual conversation

This does *not* mean shouting. Not ever. Nor does it mean speaking a level where the people immediately in front of you are wincing under the blast. You are aiming for commu-nication without intimidation.

What it does mean is a certain degree of appropriate projec-tion. The effect should be to increase the volume of your voice to about 5% more than your normal conversational level. If the audience is larger than 20 people, an increase of 10% is what you need. Beyond 50 people, you should always ensure that a microphone is available. But even if your voice is electronically amplified, maintain the 'normal plus 10%' volume. A microphone cannot create intensity for you: it can only help to enhance the intensity you have created for yourself.

Punchy, precise diction

In casual, relaxed, conversations, we run words together and it doesn't really matter. Because conversation is a two-way process, any lack of understanding can be cleared up immediately. But if someone is listening to a presentation it may be minutes (or hours!) before anything can be clarified. This means that, especially in front of groups of 20 or more, special care has to be taken with individual words. I do not want you to sound like a pedantic elocution teacher: the rain in Spain can remain firmly where it already is). You can achieve word enunciation without audience alienation.

Comprehensive Eye Contact

Eye contact is not always a good thing. It can be frightening and counter-productive. It can be used to convey either intense sexual attraction or intense dislike.

But when used carefully, eye contact is the ingredient that makes your intensity clear to most of the people, most of the time.

If you speak to a small group (less than 20 people), without making eye contact, you will come across as arrogant, shifty or very nervous. Some presenters seem to be able to look just about anywhere apart from into the eyes of the audience. They are missing the chance to really connect.

The most effective presentational eye contact is an extended glance, which lasts for no more than three seconds. This is long enough for the glanced-at individual to feel the connection, but not so long that they start to feel uncomfortable.

With a group of 20 people, you should be striving to make sure that every member of the audience receives several extended glances during the course of your presentation. Then they will all feel that you have made personal contact with them as individuals. Even when sitting among a group, everyone likes to feel that they are being treated as an individual, rather than as a part of an amorphous audience-creature.

But audience members also have this innate desire when they are sitting as part of a group of 50 or 500 people. How can you possibly make personal eye contact with such large numbers?

Here is the answer:

DON'T EVEN TRY

You should *not* be aiming for eye contact. You should be aiming for the *illusion* of eye contact.

Imagine you are on a small stage, speaking from behind a lectern which is placed towards one side of the stage. This is a very common corporate presentation scenario.

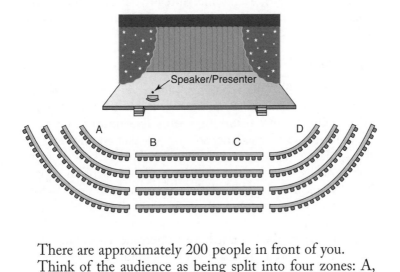

There are approximately 200 people in front of you.

Think of the audience as being split into four zones: A, B, C and D. This is where the illusion starts. If the presenter looks at someone in zone A, then approximately 10 people in his immediate vicinity will believe that *they* have been looked at. But the illusion goes further. Despite knowing that they have not been *directly* 'eye-contacted', everyone else in zone A will still feel that you have at least made an effort to include them. It is as though a pleasant wave of connectivity spreads into the audience from the point of *actual* eye contact. Everyone in the audience should realize that they cannot be treated as individuals, with constant individual contact. But they will still feel cared for if they can see that you are at least trying to bring them into your *sphere* of contact.

So far, we have only dealt with zone A. The process has to be repeated for the other zones as well. After you have glanced at a face in A for three seconds then glance at one in D, and then B … and so on.

Make your zone selection random. If you are constantly going A-B-C-D-C-B-A-B-C-D, then you will look like a Dalek playing 'Seek and Exterminate!'

Try also to include glances at people sitting in the front, middle and back of each zone. Spread your eyes around like presentational margarine, then the whole audience will be left with the taste of human contact.

High Pace

Slow and deliberate speaking can never be compelling. Lack of speed can kill communication. Humans are capable of listening to and absorbing words five times faster than we are capable of speaking, so slow speakers do not engage the speaking capacity of an audience. This lack of engagement means that the listeners have plenty of brain capacity to think of things other than your presentation. Before the end of every sentence, they may lose the will to live, let alone listen.

Don't panic. You do not have to become a speaking submachine gun. You should try to maintain an overall pace that is just slightly faster than the one you use in casual conversation. You should be just fast enough that you and your audience are aware of speed. If they can *feel* your speed, then their thoughts will be carried along by it.

Notice that we have said *overall* pace. There are some typhoon-style presenters (mainly American) who manage to maintain a remarkably compelling level of clarity when speaking at a constant 400 words per minute. For them, non-stop attack is very effective, if somewhat frightening.

The vast majority of presenters are better off using a variety of speeds for different phases of the presentation. The pace might drop significantly when you are emphasizing key points, especially when you are dealing with complex numbers. When you are presenting information that has emotional content (redundancies, news of death) it would be appropriate to slow down even more.

However, any humour or motivational segments must be pushed through with your foot hard down on the accelerator. Overall, keep your speed, but don't forget variety.

So, don't just be conversational. Use the adrenalin of the occasion to stimulate you into being an animated dinner-party guest who is so compelling that they are welcome in any dining-room, board-room or ball-room.

Control your Body

Forget about body language. As I said earlier, it has been an overblown fad for far too long. The words that you say and how they come out of your mouth are far more important than anything the rest of your body is doing.

After all, history does not remember the body language of Lincoln, Churchill or Kennedy ... but we can remember their *spoken* language.

The Mehrabian Myth has fueled the obsession with body language. Albert Mehrabian is a Professor at the University of California in Los Angeles. He carried out a series of studies in the 1960s about the relative importance of the spoken word in face-to-face communication. The results of his research are typically expressed like this:

'Only 7 per cent of the overall impact that you have in spoken communication comes from the actual words you say.'

By 'typically', I mean totally grossly inaccurately. For about 30 years, through no fault of his, Professor Mehrabian's research has been constantly misquoted.

I won't bore you with the details of the tests he carried out (no offence, Albert). But you should know that the participants were only allowed to use one word at a time ... with the only variation allowed being the tone adopted in saying those words. In fact, Mehrabian has patiently explained on many occasions that the 7% number only relates to situations where the speaker is talking about their *feelings*. He has never suggested that non-verbal factors (like body language) are more important than what you are actually saying.

So, forget about gestures. The audience doesn't worry about them so neither should you. Their minds will be on what you are saying, not what your hands are doing.

You may still be thinking:

'But what should I do with my hands?'

The only time to think about your hands is just before you open your mouth.

Learn from sportsmen.

Just before the start of a race, runners adopt a specific ready position. So do tennis players about to receive a serve. A speaker also needs a ready position. Here is what you should do:

Just as you arrive at the presentation area, just for a second, put your hands down loosely by your sides. I do mean *just for a second*. You should not be standing to attention.

Then bend your elbows so that your hands can just about touch each other at waist level ... but do *not* allow them to clasp each other.

From that planted position, you will find that hand movements will come naturally with the flow of what you say.

Or they won't.

Frankly, *it doesn't matter.* All your mental energy should be focused on your vocal chords, not your hands.

Mind you, there are some hand positions to avoid, unless you enjoy looking daft:

The Wing Commander

Hands clasped tightly behind your back, with genitals thrust forward: 'Now look here chaps, I want you to give the Luft-waffe a jolly good thrashing...'

To be avoided unless you have a huge moustache, in which case you will always look like a prat anyway.

Both Hands thrust into trousers

The pocket billiards position so thoroughly condemned by my housemaster.

Any movement in that vicinity is distracting and unpleasant.

The Teapot

One hand on hip. Too Graham Norton.

The Double Teapot

Both hands on hips. Too Flash Gordon. Without a world to save.

Arms Folded

Only good for hiding a gut or a nasty tie.

Of course, if you are using cards, one hand could be holding them ... unless you feel more comfortable with them placed on a table or lectern in front of you. Many presenters find that the feeling of a card in one hand automatically makes them feel more comfortable with the other hand. Try it.

No Bare Knuckle Presenter should ever be remembered for their gestures. As soon as you forget about your hands, so will your audience.

So ... if you can control yourself, you are giving yourself a fighting chance of controlling the reaction of your audience. Now it's time to consider how much control you can have when you enter the gladiatorial arena itself: the room in which you will actually present to the people that you want to persuade.

CHAPTER 10

CONTROL THE DAY

Despite all your research, content preparation and practicing there could still be a great deal of unpleasantness waiting for you at the presentational venue itself.

This chapter is about how to bring the techniques described in the previous chapter into actual battle conditions, as well as how to control the environment where you will be speaking.

The Environment

In order to control your environment, you have to become your own stage manager. Although a large amount of the material in this chapter relates to conference/platform presenting, the stage management ground rules apply to *all* presentations.

Control is something you must have over every aspect of what happens before, during and immediately after your presentation.

There is an endless list of potential screw-ups that can result in anything from distraction to disaster.

How Much Control Can You Have?

You should be as controlling as you can be without being seen as a pain in the arse.

Stage management can include things such as positioning of screens, stages, lecterns and audience layout, plus elements of production (timing, the use of space and getting into and out of the presentation area).

No matter what sort of presentation you are involved in, the stage management starts well before you get in front of the audience. I learned this very early on in my speaking career when my engagements were predominantly humorous After Dinner Speeches.

At a live event, the best way to ensure people laugh is to make sure that the audience are close to you and each other as well as being able to clearly see and hear you. It also helps if you can start your speech before their alcohol-enhanced state has changed from receptive to rebellious.

So, to be certain my clients got the result they wanted, I had to make sure that I got what I wanted. This often meant I had to be strong to the point of being bloody minded. I always insist that:

- no matter how large the room, the tables are packed so closely together that the waiters can only just do their job;
- I am allowed to do a full microphone check before anyone walks into the room;
- orders for after-dinner drinks are taken during the main course;
- there is a clearly announced comfort break just as coffee is served;
- every single member of the waiting staff has left the room before I am introduced;
- someone who will use the exact introduction that we have agreed on introduces me.

This apparent pedantry sometimes does not make me very popular with the organizer, but it always made me popular with the *audience*.

Your audience will evaluate your presentation on *everything* that relates to it. If they can't see or hear you, if there are distractions or if you tripped on your way to the stage it will reduce your impact. So you must get all the practicalities right.

Get the audience just where you want them

You must make sure the audience is laid out in the best possible way, unless unshakeable business convention dictates that there is nothing you can do (e.g. when you are visiting another company's boardroom).

In a great many boardrooms, the projector screen is placed in the centre of an end wall, thus guaranteeing that it is the centre of attention. In conference rooms, organizers continue to insist on bizarre seating arrangements. I often see cabaret-style roundtables for conferences when only two out of the eight people round the table can view the stage without turning their chairs or twisting their necks.

Audience seating blocks should, whenever possible, be curved in such a way as to focus everyone's attention towards the centre of the stage. It is always best not to put a central isle into a large seating block because it has the effect of removing the best seats in the house.

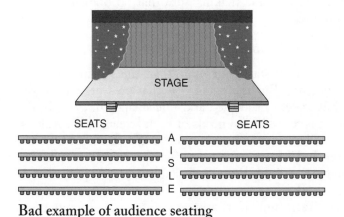

Bad example of audience seating

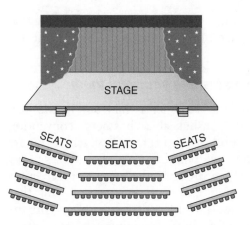

Good example of audience seating

For the best atmosphere, there should be no empty seats. Lay out just short of the right number of seats so that a late-comers' row can be created just before the start.

Have a team of people, some at the door and some at the front of the auditorium who have rehearsed the process of getting the audience to sit at the front and sit together, not leaving gaps between them. Your overall aim should be to keep your audience close and comfortably facing in the right direction while making sure that no one sits next to an empty seat.

Let there be lighting

Presenters must stand out more than the screen and more than audience. But the paradox is that presenters need the light but screens need the dark. The smaller an event is, the harder it is to fulfill the needs of both screens and speakers.

In smaller venues, there is rarely a dedicated light for the speaker and because there is often paranoia about screen visibility, the light that is available for the presenter is switched off.

I have seen (only just) a huge number of corporate presentations where the strongest light on the presenter was the light shining up from the lectern. They were thus reduced to being a voiceover for the slides while looking like the narrator from *The Rocky Horror Show*.

As long as the presenter is well lit, a little light on the audience can help to create a sense of community in the audience and a sense of connection for the presenter. But too much light on the audience can result in loss of focus on the presenter.

Check with the technical guys where the best light is and plead with them to make you the main focus of illumination rather than the screen.

The bottom line is this: it is your job as a presenter to find the best light you can and stay in it.

Make sure you can be heard

The only technical detail you need to know about microphones (or 'mikes') is where the ON/OFF button is. But don't touch it unless you really have to. Leave it to the professional sound guy who has hopefully provided it for you.

Get to the venue early enough to have a quick go on the mike provided well before the audience arrives. Just take three or four minutes doing this. Familiarity breeds confidence.

If you are using a radio microphone check that it works, without feedback, in all the places you intend to stand when you are presenting.

My advice in Chapter 9 about always speaking louder than in casual conversation still holds true, even when using a mike. It is *you*, not the mike that should generate the dinner-party intensity that I have already described.

Lectern-attached mikes are very directional, so your voice will not be captured if you turn your head severely left or right.

However, there is no need to lean forward toward the mike, as there will be a sound man sitting at a mixer desk who will make sure that you are heard when standing upright.

Hand-held mikes may make you feel like a comedian or a cabaret singer. They make it difficult for you to use notes on cards. You also need a certain amount of *arm discipline*, because this type of mike is highly directional. This means that you have to make sure that the elbow of the hand in which you are holding it is locked ... so that the mike's position never varies in relation to your mouth.

If you don't lock your elbow, you will find yourself turning your head and suddenly your voice won't be amplified any more. This sounds very frightening, but you can get over the problem with a few minutes of practice.

Stand mikes do allow you to use both hands to deal with cards. Make sure that you have adjusted the height of the stand long before you get up to speak. If a previous speaker has altered the height (aren't people selfish?), make sure that you know how to adjust the thing quickly under pressure while everyone is staring at you. You don't want to subject the audience to the horror of watching you desperately struggling with the stand with a sweaty one-wristed death grip.

A **clip-on lapel mike** should be a source of joy. Despite the nomenclature I have used, it is usually better to have it clipped to a shirt or tie. Just attach it and forget about it and make sure that you are polite to the sound guy, because he will do the rest.

Remember that lapel mikes work just as well in the toilet as they do on stage. Unless they are switched off, they can turn private conversations and situations into public events.

A lapel mike also works well in a car, especially after you have forgotten to take it off after a public appearance which is being filmed for TV during an election campaign. In any case, Gordon Brown would have been well-advised not to call the lady he had been talking to in public 'a bigot', whether or not he realized that the entire country was listening. I have already sent him a copy of this book.

N.B.: The battery packs for lapel mikes fit nicely in to the side pocket of a man's trousers. Female presenters should wear an outfit that includes a belt for the pack to be attached to.

Tripping avoidance

I have two practical suggestions:

Firstly, white tape on the walk up steps will help you see them. Just ask the production team or keep some in your bag. Apply to the fronts and edges of the steps and stage. The side edges are important because the most common mistake for a speaker exiting the stage is for them to fall off the side of the steps.

Secondly, do *not* look directly at the stage lighting in the last 60 seconds before your walk up. This will give your eyes a moment to adjust so you can see the walk up steps more clearly in the dark.

The walk-up

Where you appear from does affect the attitude of the people you are speaking to you. I recommend that you arrive from the front row of the audience. This generates an 'of the people' image while also demonstrating that you have just sat through the same stuff they have. This enhances the plausibility of any references you make to the content of earlier presentations.

Avoid ego-inflating walk-up music unless you have a very large audience and a keen sense of irony. And only if you want the audience to yawn and sneer simultaneously should you use *We Are the Champions* or *Simply the Best*. I once had the character-building experience of trying to take myself seriously in front of 1300 people who had seen me strut onto the stage accompanied by Wham singing *I'm Your Man*.

The best type of music is unidentifiable unless you are certain you want to make a big statement. I have seen a German financial director get a standing ovation from his staff for a rather drawn out entrance to *Ride of the Valkyries*. Frankly, it was rather disturbing.

Lecterns: protected or unprotected presenting?

Many well-fed presenters use a lectern as a safety-shield to stop the audience from seeing 75% of their body. As well as hiding dancing feet and beer bellies, it can give the presenter something to hold on to during the white-knuckle ride of their presentation.

Even though a lectern is the most practical device from which to deliver a script-based presentation, it can get in the way of the speaker-audience relationship.

However, as long as it is used properly, a lectern does not have to be a barrier.

If you have any chance to influence the position of a lectern, try to get it on one side of the stage or the other. This gives you the option of moving away from it and grabbing centre stage yourself if you want to.

As a fixed base
Using a full script was one of the delivery mechanisms I discussed in Chapter 7. This is certainly the most formal and traditional way of doing things and there is a real danger of you looking stiff and inaccessible when you are behind one.

But it doesn't have to be like that … *as long as you don't touch the lectern.*

Some lecterns will have a couple of small mikes built into them. Despite that, I recommend that you use a lapel mike so that you can move away if you want.

Let's say that you are using a typed-out script on paper. Fold the top left corner of each sheet so that you can grip and slide it across the lectern when you have finished with it. The top of the lectern should be wide enough for you to place two sheets side-by-side. This allows you to have the first second page available for reference without having to slide the first sheet across under pressure.

If possible, place the script on the lectern before any audience member walks into the room. Naturally, you won't be able to do this if someone else is using the lectern just before you. Either way, always have a spare copy of the script about your person at all times. Follow this advice also if you are using cards.

You will be using the *suck-and-spew* delivery method that I described in Chapter 7, and sweeping the audience with your eyes as I have recommended earlier in this chapter.

You will inevitably be drawn to grip the lectern. But don't do it ... because that will cause you to hunch over and spend too much time looking down rather than the people you are trying to persuade. Don't *ever* touch the thing, except to adjust your script. Treat the lectern as just something that happens to hold your script rather than something you are hiding behind.

Keep your hands loose and available for natural movement.

N.B. Make sure that you have a glass of still, pre-poured, room-temperature water available, either on a shelf inside the lectern, or at a table nearby.

As an anchor

If you are using cards as a delivery mechanism, an on-stage lectern can provide variety for you and your audience. Whenever I am doing a keynote to a large audience, I actually insist on a lectern being available. I deliver some of my speech from behind the lectern and some from centre stage, much closer to the audience. Sometimes I have a card in my hand; sometimes I leave them all spread out on the lectern.

In this way, I am using the lectern as an *Anchor Point*. It never gets in the way of audience contact but it does allow me to come across in a slightly different way, depending on the material I am saying at a given moment.

Frankly, I sometimes use the two or three seconds it takes for me to move between lectern and centre-stage as a bit of emergency thinking and re-adjustment time if I have just told a gag which has not got the desired response.

So a lectern can be a base for your script or an anchor for you and your notes. If you have this sort of mindset, the lectern won't be a barrier ... it will actually set you free.

PCs, controllers and pointers

In most situations, you should control your own speaker support material, preferably with a remote control. My favorite remote control has forward and back controls as well as a black-the-screen button, which gives your audience no alternative, but to look at *you*.

The easiest and most effective set up is to use a laptop connected to a large screen. If you position your laptop on a table to one side of the presentation area, you won't have to look behind you have to check that the intended slide is actually there ... something which always looks amateurish.

N.B. If you are using your laptop, you must switch off the hibernation feature or else your computer may shut down in between slides.

If you are talking an audience through a very complicated process chart a laser pointer can be useful. But do practice your wrist-control unless you want to look like a drunken Jedi Knight.

Delivery Sequence

The delivery process starts several seconds *before* you get up to speak, just as you hear yourself being introduced to the audience ... whether that introduction is merely 'So, Jane, tell us about your plan' or 'Will you please welcome, fresh from his award-winning show in Las Vegas....'

1. **Focus** totally on controlling things that are controllable at that moment:

   • Control your breathing ... slow and deep.
   • Control your body ... drop the shoulders and shake out the fingertips.
   • Control your mind ... focus on the exact words of the Beginning Spike to form a mental snowplough through the nerves.

2. **Wait** for a moment before standing. Your audience will be evaluating your arrival into the presentation area from the moment you are introduced. The way you look as you walk up makes a big statement. It maybe the only time the audience gets a side view of

you that shows your posture and the mindset behind it. A positive walk with a straight back elevated head and the hint of a smile will convey the message *I am confident, positive and I am enjoying this* ... even though none of these things may be true at that particular moment. Watch your speed as you move towards the presentation area. Too slow and it looks like nervous hesitation, too fast and you look like a game show host.

3. **Establish and maintain eye contact** with the audience from the moment that you face them. This is why you must know your few lines by heart, so there is no need for you to look down at any notes or script. And whatever delivery mechanism you are using (notes, script or auto-cue) make sure that you are looking at your audience at least 80% of the time.

4. **Let the room settle for a moment.** This moment of silence establishes your authority and convinces that audience that you are capable of leading them. It gives them the confidence to consent to you being the only person in the room who is allowed to say something. This is a moment that you should feel relaxing both you and them.

5. **Say your first line.** At last! Make sure it is the Beginning Spike you have written. Cut any rubbish interference words like 'OK', 'Right' and 'So'. Make sure that the way you say it is worthy of all the effort you have put into creating it.

6. **Use the space.** Even if bondage is your thing, don't get tied to a lectern. In large conference situations, try starting off behind one before later stepping out from behind it. This allows you to move downstage and create strikingly intimate moments with even the largest of

audiences. In meeting rooms and boardrooms it is better to stand away from the meeting/boardroom table. This will stop you bearing down on the audience and looking like a headmaster admonishing the Lower 5th.

7. **Move around only when you have a specific reason for doing so.** For instance, you may want to move to get a prop, make room for a co-presenter or because you want to flag up a different phase of your presentation. But the best practice is to find a central position where you are clearly at the centre of the audience's vision … and stick to it. Speakers who wander from side to side always look as though they are avoiding sniper fire. Presenting is not an activity where legs and lips should be used together.

8. **Vary your pace.** As I have mentioned in the previous section, a slightly faster pace than casual conversation will carry your audience along with you. This should be your default mode. But remember that you can provide a striking contrast by deliberately slowing down by 20% when you want to make a particularly important point. The slower speed allows just a little more of your private self to be visible and appreciated.

9. **Be receptive.** In front of a large audience, you cannot react to every scowl or shake of head that you see. It is best that you plough on with your pre-prepared material. But when you are presenting to less than 10 people, you should actively scan the audience to make sure that no one is reacting so badly that you have lost them totally. If someone is clearly snorting derisively in such an intimate setting, I urge you to pause assertively and politely call them out:

'Ian, I get the feeling that you're not with me on this point. Am I right?'

The very thought of doing this may make you wince a bit, but it is the only way of keeping you on track towards your Finishing Position. Ian may just need some acknowledgement and a brief piece of interaction. If you need more than a couple of minutes to sort out his negativity, calmly suggest that you should do it at the end of your presentation.

10. **Nail your End Spike.** No matter what happens, you must be able to deliver this. You will have spent a lot of time deciding on what the last words you leave them with are going to be. So learn them. And get them out of your mouth.

Answering Questions

You should always work out in advance whether you are likely to be asked questions during or after your presentation. At large conferences you may just be allocated a slot which is deliberately designed to be filled with a formal presentation and nothing else. On the other hand, the organizer may deliberately allow a few minutes for questions.

At the other extreme, if you are going to be sitting down to address to three people, you may be interrupted so frequently by constant questions, that keeping the overall flow towards your Finishing Position becomes quite a fight.

If you have a Bare Knuckle attitude, you should relish the prospect of having to answer questions, because it shows that the audience is engaged. Even if the questions seem hostile, you should be pleased that you have stimulated a response.

Unpleasant preparation

I have used this heading for two reasons. Firstly, because preparing for questions is never fun and secondly because you have to make sure that you thoroughly prepare for even the nastiest questions that you would prefer that no-one actually came out with.

There will be many situations that you know *must* involve questions. You should prepare for them by adopting the mind-set of a hyper-demanding, details obsessed, but short-attention-span audience member. This is the core question to constantly ask yourself:

'What would I be asking if I were them?'

If the answers to the above question are not obvious to you, get a colleague to help. In fact, get a colleague to help anyway. You might be so close to your subject that a potentially devastating and crushingly obvious potential query may not be obvious to *you*.

Don't skimp on this Audience Analysis (see page 19). Write out the possible questions in full so that you can show them to other colleagues who might be thus stimulated to think of even more potential unpleasantness for you.

More preparation questions to ask yourself include:

- What is the most embarrassing/challenging/appalling question that I could possibly be asked?
- What would I ask if I were deeply cynical?
- What question could expose our greatest weakness?
- What questions would I really love to be asked?
- Is there any Hard Core Content from my presentation that would be better dealt with in answer to a question?

Policy decision

Whatever the occasion, you must decide your overall policy on answering questions well before you actually perform:

'If a question is asked during the presentation itself, should I answer it immediately or ask if I can do so at the end?'

If you declare at the outset that you would like to leave questions until the end, you might sound rather weak. You will look even weaker if you make that declaration and someone still asks a question ... and possibly weaker still if you answer it.

However, if you really feel that you want to firmly encourage them to allow a delay, use assertive, but friendly language:

'It is important for me to give you a good overview of the project as quickly as possible before we get down to operational details, so I would be very grateful if we could leave your questions until the end of this initial presentation.'

In most situations, the best policy is to answer most questions as soon as they are asked. This approach has several advantages:

- It shows confidence.
- You are dealing with an issue while it is still fresh.
- You are seen genuinely engaging with the audience about their needs rather than merely pushing your own agenda in isolation.

Now you know what your Q & A strategy is, it's time to sharpen your specific tactics. They are so important that I have decided to dedicate the whole of the next chapter to them.

Chapter 11

CONTROL Q & A

The overall Bare Knuckle attitude to answering questions should be:

'Come and have a go if you think you're hard enough.'

But you should think this thought with a smile, not a snarl. You should see Question & Answer opportunities as friendly sparring rather than dangerous combat.

Delivery Guidelines

I will now give you some general guidelines before going on to describe the specific thought processes you will have to go through while actually in the throes of an answer.

1. **Always pause** before you open your mouth. It only needs to be for a second. But you should force yourself to do this even though you are bursting with eagerness to enlighten them. The pause moment will give you the time to make the first line of your answer genuinely compelling.

2. **Never patronize** the questioner by saying 'That's a really good question' or 'I am glad you asked me that'.

You will sound like a schoolteacher. There is also the strong implication that all the *other* questions that have been asked up to that point were lousy.

3. **If you don't know, say so.** Bluffing always sounds and smells bad. Your credibility is not damaged by an answer like, 'I don't know, but I will make sure I get you that information within 24 hours.'

4. **Interrupt if necessary.** Some people are incapable of asking a concise question. Instead, they do a speech with a question mark attached to the end. This bores everyone. Look for the opportunity to intervene with an attempt to ask the question for them: 'I think you are concerned as to whether this will effect our Bristol operation. Am I right?'

   If you do this with the right balance of firmness and politeness, everyone will be pleased that you have moved things along, including the questioner themselves.

5. **Escape from the obscure.** You must identify immediately whether a particular question is about a highly specialized issue that is of little interest to the majority of the audience. Keep your answer as brief as possible and politely offer to discuss the topic with the questioner on a private basis later.

6. **Re-channel hostility.** Hostility may be obvious from the pre-amble to the question: 'I can't believe that I am hearing this from someone who is only a middle manager …' or perhaps 'This is typical of your company's attitude. Surely you can't be telling us that we have to …'.

   Mind you, there also people who just sound hostile without realizing or intending it. For them, the first question in the Pub Quiz would be what the hell are you looking at?

Whether the hostility is issue- or personality-based, you must tune it out of your perception and simply answer the question as though the hostility were not present. It takes a very particular type of practiced presentational strength to do this rather than join the questioner in the pit of aggression. Calm politeness will quickly gain you a lot of respect from the rest of the audience ... and it is also the most effective weapon for defusing Mr Angry.

Whether the aggression is intentional or not, you should be pleased to know that the right Bare Knuckle attitude is not to fight fire with napalm. Re-channelling hostility involves a polite sidestep instead of a fist in the face.

7. **Beware dialogue.** This can't be right, surely? Isn't dialogue a good thing to have? Yes ... as long as you don't allow it to become a dictator.

Imagine a situation where you have answered a question, but the questioner keeps coming back for more. If you are making a pitch for business and the ultra-persistent participant is the chief executive, then that would be fine.

But if you are speaking to a larger audience, perhaps with a diverse range of interests, you cannot afford one person to hijack your performance. If the rest of the audience feels that your presentation has become a one-to-one conversation, they will feel excluded.

If you can feel this happening, you have to be prepared to take firm but polite control:

'David, I can see this is an important area for you, but I think it's time I moved on, because I have a lot of other ground still to cover.'

You certainly don't want the positive effect of a well-crafted and punchily delivered set-piece presentation to be horribly diminished by an ill-judged response to a tough question, or worse….to a straightforward one.

I will now give you three simple formulae that will ensure that you will always be battle-ready for pressure questioning.

The FIR Formula

You need a simple formula for organizing your thoughts … something that you can immediately access, no matter what pressure you are under. And here it is:

Face-up.

Illustrate.

Round off.

Let's look at these three phases as they are used in response to a rather mundane question.

The **Face-Up** is a sentence that immediately states a headline view on the issue raised by the question. You are immediately facing up to what the questioner wants to know.

Question: What did you have for breakfast this morning?

Face-up: I had a massively unhealthy, fat-laden, full English fry-up.

This Face-Up has certain characteristics:

- It answers the question head-on, without any hint of evasion.
- It uses distinctive phrasing rather than obvious, flat words.
- It is interesting enough for the audience to want to know more.
- It shows a hint of emotional as well as factual content

Essentially, the Face-Up is the Q & A equivalent of a Spike. It should be sharp enough to engage your questioner and make them feel that you are welcoming their probe.

The **Illustrate** phase should respond comprehensively to the hunger that the Face-Up has encouraged:

'It consisted of smoky bacon, runny fried eggs and over-done sausages, mopped up by burnt white toast sopping with butter and marmalade.'

Without wishing to celebrate my humble repast as a piece of culinary pornography, I have nevertheless injected a great deal of distinctly Bare Knuckle attitude in the way I have illustrated my answer:

- The ingredients in the illustration were comprehensive but finite.
- The language is striking enough to give the listener an immediate picture of my coronary-on-a-plate.
- What could have been a boring list is conveyed as something with colour and life.

But there is still something missing. If the answer just stopped there, the questioner might be left in doubt as to whether you have actually said all you wanted to say. Hence the need to **Round-Off:**

'For me, a traditional cooked breakfast is the only way to start the day.'

These are quite clearly my last words on the subject ... until I am asked the next question.

The Round-Off should:

- briefly echo the face-up, without being an exact repeat;
- not try to cover new territory that hasn't been in the Illustration phase;
- undoubtedly indicate that you have come to an end that you are comfortable with.

The SSS Formula

You may sometimes find yourself in situations where there is a degree of time pressure, for instance a radio interview. It is possible that the relatively leisurely FIR formula may not give you the necessary mental edge. Perhaps it doesn't quite get you to the point quickly enough.

This is when the Black Belt version is more appropriate:

Say it

Support it

Shut it

The phrase Say It is meant to imply that you should get to the point even faster with your very first words. The Support It phase should also be seen as somewhat more express in its intent than Illustrate.

Shut It has a clear double meaning:

* Shut off the topic in a relatively abrupt and sharp way.
* Simply: shut your mouth!

Let's say you are a politician being interviewed about the future of Britain's strategic defence:

Question: Can a country as small as ours really afford to buy a replacement for Trident?

Say It: Failing to buy a Trident replacement would be criminally irresponsible.

Support It: We would be perceived as a Second Division country, constantly open to blackmail by a nuclear-armed dictatorships.

Shut It: Essentially, we can't afford **not** to replace Trident.

Overall, you can see the SSS formula has more of an edge of combat than FIR. It encourages you to have a punchier mindset, as if you were quickly jabbing the questioner in the face:

Question: How can you possibly maintain your market share in the current climate?

SSS Answer: Because we still have a product that is starkly more effective than the competition.

Our brushes are hard, light and very durable ... and we know exactly how to make those qualities clear to our customers.

In fact, we are sure that we will actually increase our market share this year.

The Pause and Spike Formula

You should get into the habit of deciding whether measured and calm FIR approach is appropriate to the circumstances, or whether you should adopt the more in-your-face SSS style. Of course, you can switch from one to the other as the situation progresses. You should never feel stuck in either mode.

However, it is possible that you have the sort of mind that finds even the relatively simple three-letter acronyms to be too much of a strain to remember and act on under pressure. In fact, you may feel that you would prefer that your word-stream is not inhibited by such a precise structure.

No problem! I can give you an even simpler approach that will sharpen your overall performance without stifling your natural flow:

Pause ... Spike ... Spike

This formula just deals with the way you begin and end your answer. It asks you to spend about two seconds in silent, but focused contemplation of what you are going to say as your very first words ... despite the urge you may feel to blurt something out almost before the questioner's last words have left their mouth.

173

This will allow you to make your first sentence a truly worthwhile and striking spike, rather than merely a piece of instant blandness.

Question: Do you approve of Grammar Schools?

Bland Answer: Yes, I certainly approve of them.

This is not a Spike. It is a damp cloth. If you actually think: Pause … Spike, then you will be better placed to create something that is far more compelling:

'I think Grammar Schools are an essential part of the social fabric of this country, so I approve of them very much indeed.'

This response is a long way from bland. It has the effect of immediately making you sound like a person of authority, with specific and robust views. Incidentally, this is the sort of person that radio and TV stations love to have as guests.

And Finally …

You must control Q & A rather than letting it control you. There must come a time when you decide that it has to come to an end. You must not end your presentational performance with Q & A.

When there has been extensive and vigorous Q & A, this is nearly always a good result because it shows that the audience has shown a certain level of intellectual and emotional engagement.

But consider the following situation. You are a consultant who is recommending a particular investment strategy to a syndicate of bankers. You have delivered a 10-minute presentation that has culminated in an End Spike:

'If you stay invested in Hungary, your overall profits will dip by 20 per cent this year … and you will then have to pull out of other countries as well.'

There is then an intense 10-minute period during which your conclusions are ruthlessly probed and questioned. You eventually become aware that they have run out of questions. You should avoid the following, horribly common closing remark:

'Well, if you've got no more questions, thanks very much for your time. Just let me know if we can do anything else.'

This sort of vanilla blandness means that the audience are left with nothing memorable from you. Worse than that, they could also be left with the content of your last answer, which may not have been one of your very best. Essentially, you have given up too much control.

No problem. You can grab it back ... by concluding the Q & A with a *second* End Spike:

'We are available at any time if you need to clarify anything else. But please remember that, if you want to protect your overall European business, pulling out of Hungary immediately is something you have to urgently consider.'

The wording of this *second* End Spike deliberately echoes that of the *first* without being a straight repeat. It benefits the audience by re-emphasizing a necessary course of action. And it benefits you because you have wrestled back control and given them a lasting impression of your presentational leadership.

Chapter 12

RAISE A SMILE

Here are some horrible pieces of really *bad* advice, which I include both to frighten you and to get your humour muscles twitching just a little:

- *A sense of humour is a sign of weakness. Moments of light relief always reduce the strength of your message. No audience will take you seriously if they enjoy listening to you. Of course, the words 'enjoy' and 'presentation' should never appear in the same sentence.*

- *Have a favourite joke that you always use in every speech. This increases the chance of your audience having heard it before. They will relish the opportunity to mouth the punch line before you get to it.*

- *There is no such thing as 'unsuitable' humour. Something is either funny or it isn't. Some people are just far too sensitive. Don't waste time carefully calculating whether a particular gag is a disaster waiting to happen.*

- *Start with a long joke. Ensure that it is unrelated to the content of your presentation. If it's worked before the joke will always work, no matter what the audience (see 'unsuitable humour'). The audience will certainly remember you.*

Especially if the joke doesn't get a laugh. Or they've heard it before. Or they want you to get straight to the point.

- *Laugh at your own jokes. Wait about five seconds after your punch line before making an explosive sound from the back of your throat. This acts as a cue for the audience. The more charitable among them will feel obliged to join in to cover up any general embarrassment.*

- *Use inside jokes that mean something to only a tiny percentage of people in the room. Those privileged few will feel very special indeed. Everyone else will be intrigued as they witness this ritual from the outside: a sort of presentational Masonic handshake.*

- *The old ones are the best. Jokes are like wine. The older they get, the more memorable they are. Don't bother with fresh, untamed material. Audiences like to feel familiar with humour. So, vintage appeal is preferable to topical uncertainty.*

- *I have always enjoyed the one about Stanley Baldwin, Ramsey MacDonald and Oswald Mosely walking into a pub ....*

That's enough of the bad stuff. Sanity is on its way, firstly provided by Oscar Wilde:

'Humour is like caviar: don't spread it around like marmalade.'

Oscar was almost right. Humour is actually a deadly weapon disguised as a box of sweets. It can charm, entertain and persuade your audience. It can stimulate laughter, admiration and standing ovations. But it can also upset, offend and anger. At its worst, humour can make people hate your company, your products and *you.*

By 'humour' I mean any words that are used to make the audience smile or laugh. In a wedding or After Dinner Speech, the sole measure of success is the level of audience amusement attained. In a business speech, humour is only successful if it amuses your audience *and* it helps you to get to your desired Finishing Position.

You have to make sure that being funny is not the main characteristic you are remembered for. As you leave the room, the audience's memory capacity should ideally be filled with fond thoughts of your Micro-Statement and supporting Key Elements. Laughter should therefore only be generated with mean efficiency in a serious presentation.

The three keys to successful use of humour are:

1. Careful selection;

2. Clever blending;

3. Assertive delivery.

1 and 2 may both involve an element of writing, combined with the introduction of previously used material

Firstly, here are the six main categories of laugh-producing weapons:

The story

Two businessmen were walking through the jungle. Suddenly they see an enormous, ferocious lion roaring towards them. The first man calmly opens his briefcase, takes out a pair of running shoes and starts to put them on.

'What on earth are you doing?' said the second man. 'You can't possibly run faster than the lion.'

'Oh yes' said the first man 'but I only need to run faster than you'.

The general format is a narrative, building up tension which is eventually released by a punchline ('I only need to run faster than you'). There is nothing particularly amusing about the build up: the audience will only laugh at the end of the story. This means that you have to invest a significant amount of time before getting the return you want, i.e. laughter. If you don't get a laugh, both you and your audience will feel very uncomfortable that your investment has crashed.

This is the main drawback of the story-joke: you just *have* to get a big laugh.

The second drawback is the strong possibility of familiarity. The Lion story is so old that it was originally written in Sanskrit. If a story has a degree of antiquity, there is a good chance that some of the audience will have heard it before. You might even hear someone muttering the punch line before you get to it. This leads to bladder-loosening embarrassment for everyone. So, you must be particularly careful of stories that are too long or smell too much of déjà vu.

On the whole, story-jokes are best left for after-dinner speeches. You should have total certainty about the real value of a story-joke before including it in a business speech. Remember the problem of familiarity. Good stories are usually *old* stories. They are usually long enough for audience members who have heard them before to realize that fact.

The only way of combating this is to make sure that *your* version of the story is quite brilliant: brilliantly told *and* brilliantly edited.

Look at each story written out in full. Take a red pen and cross out all the words that are not absolutely necessary. Cut the word count right down to the marrow. Think of the story as an elegant sprint to the punch line.

Then learn it. Word for word. Like a poem. Every single word. This will be very painful. But you *must* be able to tell the story without any ums, errs or you knows. And without hesitation, deviation or repetition. After all, you have a demanding live audience to answer to. It is this level of confident delivery that gives the audience confidence to laugh.

In fact, if you are going to use *any* of the types of humorous material I mention in this chapter, it is essential that you learn the constituent words so well that you cannot possibly get any of them wrong under pressure.

And forget about reading it from a script. No matter how short or long the joke, it simply won't come to life in your mouth if you have to pick it up from a piece of paper.

The story has to be told with total confidence, total conviction and total efficiency. Only then does it have a chance of getting a laugh.

You can probably include two story-gags in a five-minute speech. Absolutely no more. Listening to a story-gag, even a good one being told well, is a big drain on the audience's stamina … so don't push it.

The one- or two-liner

'I have already spoken in front of the Prince of Wales, the Duke of Gloucester and many other public houses too numerous to mention'.

In the space of a very few words, the one/two liner makes the audience think in one direction, and then quickly *switches* the direction. The more severe the switch, the bigger the laugh, as in this classic Barry Cryer gag:

'I don't like sport. I'm actually in AA. Its an organization called Athletics Anonymous: every time I feel like taking some exercise, I phone them up and someone comes round and drinks with me until the feeling goes away.'

Okay, I know the above gag is more than two lines long. But it fulfils the key criterion: the gag gets to the point and gets to the laugh in under 10 seconds.

You can tell four or five one-liners in the time it takes to tell one story-joke. So the time used/laughter produced ratio is more favourable.

The other advantage of this type of gag is that if it doesn't get a laugh, you can quickly move on with the minimum of discomfort. The audience will forget very quickly that the gag didn't work. However, if a story-joke disappears down the pan, the audience will remember it for the next six months.

But there is also a significant downside. If you use too many one-liners, you will sound like a comedian, not a chief executive.

They are also fiendishly difficult to write. The really effective one-liner has a biting precision which is beyond the pen of everyone but the professional scriptwriter. Perhaps you can prove me wrong. If you can, please write some of them for me: you can find my contact details at the end of the book.

The general topical reference

The topical gag is funny for only a short period of time. It must refer to something in the news which will be immediately recognized by the audience. The two examples below had a topical shelf-life of about 12 months, but their funniness has now faded away with the passage of time:

'I should have been doing a speech for Arthur Andersen today, but somebody shredded my contract'.

The formula is easy to see. You mention an entity which is in the news and then you *exaggerate* its best-known characteristic in an unusual context:

'I've been asked to the annual dinner of the Lada User's Association. The invitation says 7:30 for 11'.

Do be careful about defamation. I don't intend to give a detailed exposition of the laws of libel, even though I could then have charged a lot more for the book. However, it is always safe to joke about the characteristics of public figures:

'Gordon Brown is such a dour politician. He can light up the House of Commons simply by walking out of it'.

The local topical reference

This is a gag that is only funny for *that* audience at *that* time.

I once spoke to a group of managers from an IT company, at the same hotel where another part of the company had stayed the previous week. This other group had actually been ejected from the hotel because of behaviour that had ranged from drunkenness to criminal damage:

'I had an interesting journey here. At Leicester railway station I had to fight through a mob that was vomiting on the street and throwing furniture through windows. Apparently, it was a training seminar for your sales force'.

Not very funny now, you may think. You are right. But at the time, it was such a bull's-eye that the chief executive led a standing ovation *just for that gag.*

Another time I spoke at a dinner hosted by a car company on HMS Britannia, which is moored in a harbour near Edinburgh. As a surprise start to the dinner, a local actor performed 'The Address to the Haggis'. Unfortunately, his face was painted in a way that the Scottish bard would have found rather garish. And so:

> *'I very much enjoyed the dinner. For me, the major highlight was seeing Robbie Burns made up as Adam Ant'.*

I will never be able to use that gag again. But it got the biggest laugh of the evening.

An audience feels really flattered if you have clearly made the effort to craft a gag just for them. If the speaker has gone to that trouble, he must be worth listening to. A good inside joke means that you are less likely to be treated like an outsider.

However, this does not mean you should tell lawyer jokes to lawyers (similarly with accountants, doctors, estate agents). Every lawyer has heard every lawyer joke, especially that really clever one someone e-mailed to you the other day.

The insult

Wow, doesn't that sound like a dangerous word? Surely this is far too risky for a corporate presentation.

Well, perhaps. Remember that *botulinum* toxin is a poison, but used in small doses, it can make you look really good (this sentence probably wins the Most Strained Analogy of the Chapter Award).

An insult is only funny if it is not rude or offensive. It must, however, be pointed:

> *'John is a man with a joke for every occasion, and I've enjoyed hearing it again today'.*

The target of the gag must be someone who is well known to the vast majority of the audience. Ideally, the gag should exaggerate a well-known characteristic:

> *'When Frank goes on holiday, he takes a £5 note and a pair of underpants – and he doesn't change either of them'.*

You have to be sure that the target is a strong enough personality to withstand the humour. If they have a high enough profile within the organization, they will usually be flattered by the attention. I know many corporate egos that would only be dented if they were *not* targeted in a speech.

Make sure that the gag is not innately cruel. You can joke about someone's waistline if they are a couple of pounds over-weight, but not if they need their own postcode.

Never imply that the target is bad at their job. But you can have a little fun at the expense of their credentials, without trying to damage them:

> *'David is the country's leading expert on website design. In fact, he's just finished his second book and he's going to start colouring his third tomorrow'.*

The best insult gags tickle their targets with a feather, rather than rupturing them with a spear. Essentially, they are gags that the individuals concerned not-so-secretly would love to have told about them.

Quotations

Don't use them. If they are any good they will have been used thousands of times by speakers who are not nearly as good as you. When a speaker uses a quote it just shows that he can't think of anything useful to say himself.

The only exception is where the quote is very funny or very appropriate ... like the brilliantly chosen one at the beginning of this chapter (modesty is so tedious).

If you've got something to say, you will probably say it better than someone who died 100 years ago. Or perhaps George Bernard Shaw really did know more about your company than you do.

Careful Selection

So, where do you get funny material? There are actually several answers:

1. Write it yourself

Oh yeah, sure. I'm an accountant, for God's sake.

Hmmm. Fair point. Humorous speaking has been a large part of my life for 20 years. However, I am to gag-writing what the Serious Fraud Office is to convictions

Forget it. Creating the stuff with a pen and blank piece of paper is something you just don't have time for, apart from the occasional topical reference as mentioned above.

2. Buy joke books

They are all crap. And I do mean all of them. I have bought hundreds in the last two decades. One gag in a thousand is useful. If you have the patience to go through them, you have my unstinting admiration, even though you clearly have no personality.

3. Joke websites

I have found over 50 sites on the net which consist entirely of lawyer jokes. The standard is appalling and there is an enormous overlap between sites.

If you type the word 'joke' into any search engine, the results you get will delight and sicken you. You will be delighted by the sheer number of sites listed. You will be sickened by the poor quality.

But it is worth ploughing through some of them— especially the ones that have their own internal search engines. If you desperately need a gag on a particular topic you may find a gem. But it's likely to be quartz.

4. Writers

Good, consistent writers are as easy to find as unicorns. I found one once, lurking in the cafeteria of Thames Television. I loved the stuff he wrote. But then he politely explained that he couldn't write for me because he was too busy writing for Steve Coogan and Rory Bremner, whoever they are.

If you also have the budget, try approaching the Comedy Writers Association (phone 01322 710742). Get some writers to send you some samples. See if you can strike a rapport with one. If the two of you click, your union will be blessed with the laughter of many audiences.

5. Your ears

Keep them open at all times. If you hear or read something funny, write it down. Immediately and absolutely verbatim. Do not leave anything out.

Build up you own humour file of favourites: gags that become your best friends.

Don't be proud. Many corporate speeches have been spiced up by the content of *Reader's Digest*.

Remember this: if you steal from one person, it's theft. If you steal from a hundred people, it's research. I can't remember where I researched that one.

Moral Note

Unless you have an innate talent for writing them, you have got to be able to *find* gags somewhere.

You need to have access to a file of funny material that has been used before and can be used again.

I don't necessarily mean stuff that has already been used by *you*. Make a habit of going to formal dinners. Watch comedians in Las Vegas or Blackpool. Make yourself as sensitive as possible to the potential of humour that you read and hear.

I am *not* suggesting wholesale theft, although I don't think that Jimmy Tarbuck would be really upset if you used a couple of his gags. Once a joke has been told in public, it is legally deemed to be in the public domain, and it is very difficult for the originator to enforce any form of ownership. However, it would be a different story if you were daft enough to lift whole routines from a well-know comedian and started to perform them yourself. If you decide to do that, keep the number of your solicitor handy by the phone.

There is certainly a staggering array of comedy available on DVD. *You Tube* is also a superb source.

However, even when you witness a whole evening comic brilliance, you will know that perhaps only two or three of the lines you hear could possibly be used effectively by you. You are unlikely to be able to re-create the delivery style of Jimmy Carr.

Watching comedians and other After Dinner Speeches will stimulate you to *think* in the right way. You may hear some lines that spark off a fruitful burst of creativity ('Interesting idea ... if the character in that story had been an estate agent, then maybe ...').

Types of Humour to Avoid

- racism;
- sexism;
- cartoons;
- impersonations;
- infatuations.

A badly chosen joke can lurch unhelpfully between you and your audience like an uninvited drunk.

Racism, Sexism and Cartoons

Racism is not funny and it never has been. And sexism is something which upsets many chicks.

Dilbert cartoons are a very popular visual aid. Popular and dangerous. Using cartoons like this is a gross breach of copyright (more free legal advice). Scott Adams (the creator of *Dilbert*) is very rich and can afford lawyers who are much better than me. In every country.

Irrespective of the legalities, even self-created cartoons look puerile. If you can't make them laugh with your voice, you certainly won't make them laugh with a marker pen.

Impersonations

They are very difficult. This is why Rory Bremner gets paid ridiculous amounts of money. Actually, they are also not very funny unless the script is brilliant. Have you seen Mike Yarwood recently?

In fact, any material that requires you to put on a different voice should be avoided. Using a false accent is a very good way of looking very stupid indeed.

Infatuations

Don't fall in love with a joke. Unrequited adoration is always tragic. I will now tell you my favourite joke. It was written (and delivered many times) by the late Willie Rushton, one of the finest British After Dinner speakers of the late 20th century:

'I was sitting in my hotel room and I saw a menu which said

'Room Service – Any Time'

So I phoned them up and said 'I'd like scrambled eggs on toast, please .... during the Renaissance''

This is a gag of unparalleled intellectual brilliance. However, if I try to tell it, it never gets a laugh. It probably never will. It's just too damned clever. Because I am so infatuated with the gag, I keep trying to use it. One day I will come to my senses and accept that it just doesn't love me. You can try it for yourself ... and if you get your audiences to laugh at it, I will be very upset indeed.

Careful Blending

Your overall attitude should always be that you are a serious Bare Knuckle Presenter who happens to have a good sense of humour. You definitely do not want to come across as a comedian who just happens to be doing a serious presentation.

Blending involves looking carefully through your Baseline Text and seeing whether there is a genuine opportunity for injecting a laugh. By 'genuine', I mean not forced. If you force humour into a place where it doesn't belong, it can sound like the clang of a cracked bell. You will be remembered more for your crassness than your clear thinking.

The concept of blending is best explained by looking at some examples in various different contexts.

A fund manager client of ours was making a presentation to an industry conference about the economic prospects for his geographical region. After he had finished a section that respectfully disagreed with much mainstream opinion, he included the following comment:

'I've always respected economists: after all, they have correctly predicted nine out of the last three recessions'.

Of course, this is a gag that has a certain amount of antiquity. But the context provided the perfect opportunity for our client to blow off the dust and put it into action. The line nicely reinforced the views he has expressed as well as getting a significant laugh.

In the next example, the chief executive of a large company was doing a speech to mark the retirement of a senior colleague. He cleverly made use of the fact that both his wife and his ex-wife (who remained good friends) were in the audience:

'Well, we all know that behind every successful man, there stands an astonished woman ... in Frank's case, TWO astonished women!'

This got a huge laugh at the same time as delighting all three individuals encompassed by the joke.

Finally, here is a situation where an MP has made clever use of the fact that he was a last-minute replacement at a business lunch for a rather better-known speaker than him:

'You can always tell how highly you are rated as a speaker by how long before the event you are asked to speak.

International Statesmen, of the calibre of Gorbachev and Kissinger are often approached 18 months in advance.

Former British Cabinet ministers might need SIX months notice.

You might be able to book a reasonably well-known national TV celebrity with four WEEKS warning.

On the other hand, you can probably get a local public figure or clergyman if you have the courtesy to let them know a couple of DAYS before your event.

So...it was with enormous pleasure...that I received your Chairman's phone call at 6.30 this morning.'

The words in block capitals were the ones that had to be emphasized in delivery. The overall effect was that the speaker was seen as an amusing good sport who didn't take his own status too seriously ... quite an unusual asset for a politician.

Assertive Delivery

Humour must be delivered:

- with precision;
- with confidence;
- with speed;
- with practice.

Precision

There are hundreds of ways to phrase a gag wrongly. There are probably only one or two ways to phrase it correctly.

Calculate the precise wording. Learn it and stick to it. Humour is a delicate creature: if you get one word wrong, it will probably die. This is because jokes (of whatever length) must be constructed with almost mathematical precision, like a house of cards. Using the wrong word in the build up is like suddenly pulling a card away. The whole thing collapses before the punch line is delivered.

So treat every gag like a sacred text: used precisely it will lead you to the Holy Grail of laughter.

Confidence

You can have no doubts. You can only use a gag that you *know* is funny. An audience can sniff lack of confidence from a hundred yards away. If there is even a hint that you are not sure about the gag, you will achieve a crushing silence, or patronizingly polite smiles. You will be able to hear a mosquito clearing its throat.

You know what I think about quotes. However, Henry Ford once said:

'If you think you can or you think you can't, then you are probably right.'

I hope that he was actually talking about telling jokes at the time. Total conviction is essential: no guts, no glory.

Speed

I don't necessarily mean high speed. Not all the time, anyway. But there can be no stumbles or hesitation as you drive towards the pay-off line.

There is no room for this sort of hesitation:

'This accountant walks into a bar ... no ... he was an investment banker ... and it was actually a restaurant ... anyway ...'

I am not suggesting that you should sprint through the gag ... merely that you increase your pace of delivery by about 5% from that of casual conversation (i.e. just a smidgeon faster than you would deliver non-funny presentational material. The necessary speed is very hard to describe in print, but easy to recognize when you hear it ... or achieve it yourself.

The only way to get the knack of gauging the right pace when you really need it is revealed by the next heading below.

Practice

More than any other type of presentational performance, humour delivery is a sport ... and one that should be played a great deal in private before you unleash your skills on an unsuspecting public.

I have already told you that there are relatively few ways to phrase a gag. Well, there are even fewer ways to deliver one. In a way that gets a laugh, that is. Practice your precise, confident and pacey delivery into a hand-held tape recorder. Experiment by emphasizing different words (as in the MP's opening gag above).

Eventually, you will get to the stage where you have practiced a given gag so much, that it doesn't seem funny any more. That is when you and your material are ready for combat.

CHAPTER 13

ADAPT TO AFTER DINNER

If someone asks you to do an After Dinner Speech, don't hesitate. *Refuse.*

There is more opportunity for disaster in an After Dinner Speech than in any other form of spoken communication. Olympic athletes, Oscar-winning actors, top comedians and cabinet ministers are all capable of doing very bad After Dinner Speeches. If you are not up to it, you just shouldn't do it. This is a context where the fight for audience attention can be particularly brutal.

I have done more than 2000 After Dinner Speeches, so I have a very clear grasp of this arena. The difficulties of After Dinner Speaking are so intense that I have decided to devote a whole chapter to them rather than merely inserting a section in one of the Challenging Situations chapters towards the end of the book.

This activity is so demanding because of two unique problems of the After Dinner situation. The first problem lies in the correct assessment of the Finishing Position: the realistically desirable result that you want to achieve.

When a professional entertainer performs an After Dinner Speech he has one, very clear desired outcome: he wants the audience to laugh almost continuously for as long as he is speaking. If he were to think in terms of a Finishing Position, it would be:

> *'At the end of my speech, I want the audience to feel good about having laughed for 45 minutes.'*

This is the purest possible Finishing Position for an After Dinner Speech, untarnished by any business concerns.

But if you are a chief executive, the chairman of an association or some form of visiting dignitary (perhaps athletic or political), then your task is inevitably more complex. Just making the audience feel good from laughter is not good enough on its own.

Or is it? You see, the second problem is one of timing and environment. At 10.00pm, after a four-course meal including half a bottle of wine, no one has a desire to be subjected to serious content. If they wanted a message, they would listen to their voicemail.

Here is another statement to add to the collection of things you will *never* hear an audience member say. Here is the After Dinner version:

> *'I thought the Chief Executive was too funny for my liking. That speech may have been very entertaining, but I wanted more about his strategic vision. At this time of night, I want to hear details'.*

After Dinner is the worst possible time for conveying any serious information. Expecting an After-Dinner audience to absorb anything serious is unrealistic and just plain rude. I have *never* seen a dinner enhanced by a serious speech, but I have seen many dinners ruined by one.

But what if you don't have the '*I must do a serious speech*' problem? What if you want to do a speech that is just meant to be funny and nothing else?

Well, here is more bad news. Writing and delivering an After Dinner Speech that is focused only on generating laughter is even *more* difficult. In other types of presenting, the purpose of any humour is to drive home the Micro-Statement so that the audience gets to the Finishing Position. The laughter then only has to be moderate in intensity. But when you are *only* trying to stimulate laughter, then the laughs have to be very strong indeed.

You have probably had to sit through some pretty bad After Dinner Speeches. And, let me guess, if you are reading this chapter you could well be *dreading* the prospect of having to do one yourself, even if you are an experienced business presenter.

I am delighted by your terror. This means that there is some hope for you. You must use the terror to force you to prepare.

Should you actually do it?

You will nearly always get several weeks' notice that you have to do an After Dinner Speech. However, someone may sneak up to you at a dinner and unexpectedly whisper in your ear a request to perform. I unashamedly repeat the advice I gave at the beginning of this chapter:

JUST SAY NO.

All the best After Dinner Speeches have been written long in advance of their delivery. Most of the crap ones were written at short notice or not really written at all ('I prefer just to scribble a few notes on the back of the menu and wait for the liqueurs to inspire me'). Don't be tempted by the siren voice of spontaneous laziness. The twinge of embarrassment you feel from giving a polite but firm refusal is nothing compared to the agony you could cause by delivering an After Dinner Disaster. I mean agony for everyone at the dinner, not just you.

Have I scared you enough yet? I don't think so. Let's now consider the nature of the potential horror.

You are a director/senior manager/well-known-figure-in-the-industry. You have attended your company's one-day senior management conference, from 10am to 5pm. Apart from the lunch break, a token Q & A session at the end, and a mildly amusing couple of gags from the sales director (who is a bit of a 'character'), it has been unremitting assault by a platoon of PowerPoint ninjas.

There is scheduled free time between 5pm and 7pm ('free' means 'uninvoiceable').

At 7pm, there is a drinks reception and dinner will sit down at 8pm. If you are lucky.

At most conference venues, it is extremely likely that no one will get any food before 8.15pm. Any speech making is unlikely to start before 9.45pm. 10.15pm is more likely. 10.30pm is a horribly distinct possibility.

You have been asked to speak after the meal. You are also considered to be quite a 'character'. Or you are the chief executive (these two concepts are mutually exclusive).

Some questions to ask:

Question: Why should there be a speech at all at this time of night?

Probable Answer: The Chief Executive always does one.

or

We always get someone from the Industry to speak.

Question: Are the speeches always received well?

Probable Answer: Err … well … err … sometimes.

Just because someone 'always' does a speech in this slot is not a good enough reason in itself. So here are the crucial questions:

What *should* the After Dinner Speech achieve?
What *will* it achieve?

These are two questions where you need the answer to be the same.

If there have been presentations all day, then *surely* all possibly useful information has already been conveyed. In fact, the audience has probably been given far more information than it can possibly absorb. Even sponges reject water once they are completely saturated.

They may well be enjoying the opportunity to talk with colleagues over their chicken and Chateau Conference wine. But they switched off from listening mode at 5pm. Any attempt at a serious speech will be met with a wall of indifference, boredom or even anger. No one will change their opinion about your e-marketing plan at 10.30pm.

The Approach – If You Really Have To

Despite reading what I have said, you still might have come to this sort of conclusion:

> 'But, look here, I agree with what you say, but I just have to do a speech then, damn it. People expect me to. And I can't just tell a string of gags. I am not a stand-up comic. I am a chief executive. I just don't do jokes. That's what consultants are for.'

Oh well, time for some consultancy. I do accept that, despite the strident view I have already expressed, senior executives sometimes *have* to make an After Dinner Speech. Whether the audience wants one or not. Sometimes it is impossible to fight corporate inertia.

I reluctantly admit that there is a possible compromise. Here it is:

> **The speech should essentially be an entertaining one, but with a very tight Micro-Statement, so that the serious stuff makes up less than 20% of the content.**

Let's split up the Key Elements of the preceding statement.

- entertaining – I do mean funny. You do need gags. Lots of them.

- very tight Micro-Statement – I mean that it must have Neanderthal simplicity. The later the hour, the less complexity is appropriate.

197

- less than 20% of the content – Yes, I do mean only 60 seconds of a five-minute speech. This is an absolute maximum.

'But I have heard loads of After Dinner speeches that don't abide by those guidelines. They have usually got far more serious content than that'.

I am sure you have. But did you enjoy listening to them? Really?

If you can get solid laughs for four minutes and leave them with a Micro-Statement that they can remember the next day, then you will be treated like a God.

Well, you should be.

In Chapter 3, I said that any humour should relate to the Micro-Statement, and that you should only use humour that helps to *emphasize* the Micro-Statement.

Well, I have some good news. When it comes to After Dinner speaking, you can ignore all that. The humour doesn't have to have anything to do with the Micro-Statement. Your funny stuff should *only* be there to get laughs. It must be strong enough to have life independent of the micro-statement.

I will now deal with the type of material to use and the structure of the speech.

Writing The Damn Thing

Naturally, I still recommend that you use the **Preparation Pipeline** ... but with an After Dinner attitude. This means that you should not spend as much intellectual and emotional energy on the Micro-Statement and supporting Key Elements. Your serious material should be cleverly superficial, rather than deeply profound.

Structure

The structure of an After Dinner Speech can be much looser than the serious, daytime presentation. There is not the same requirement for the audience to remember your Key Elements for the next day. You do not have to think in terms of persuasion to retain information. But you do have to think in terms of maximizing the amount of possible laughter. To do this, you should use most of your strongest material close to the beginning of your speech.

I can feel you resisting this concept. After all, shouldn't you build up to your best stuff? Slowly get the audience on your side, warm them up and *then* hit them with your solid gold?

Frankly, NO.

Attention spans decrease exponentially for every minute past 9.30pm that the speeches start. I do not have a shred of mathematical evidence to support this. But I do have 20 years of sometimes bitter experience. This has occasionally involved reminding the organizer that it would be nice to get the speeches finished before the room has to be set for breakfast.

It is rarely advisable to start your speech on one day and finish it the next.

Start Fast

You have to be funny *immediately*. If you don't get them laughing at the start, then *you never will*.

This is how your speech should look, in terms of strength of your material:

Beginning	Middle	End
STRONG	VERY	WEAKER
STRONG	STRONG	STRONG
STRONG		VERY STRONG

The stuff that you know is weakest should be slipped in between 50% and 80% into the speech. This is also the best place to put in any Micro-Statement. If you really must. If you have shown them the courtesy of entertaining them for a few minutes then it is likely that they will show *you* the courtesy of listening to your Micro-Statement. But make it quick – and get back to the entertainment as soon as possible.

Andrew Corlett, then President of the Isle of Man Law Society, used this type of structure superbly at the Society's dinner in November 2004. The majority of his speech is pasted below. I have inserted comments to show how he adapted the Bare Knuckle method.

When we started to create the speech, he told me that the Knockout Result he wanted was for the audience to briefly hear about his vision for the future of the Island ... and for them to have quite a few laughs at the same time. This was an entirely realistic aim, so it was immediately adopted as his desired Finishing Position.

Instead of relying on stories, his main weapons were one- and two-liners, cleverly adapted to include characters that were well known to the audience.

'Your Excellency, Your Honours, Chief Minister, Ministers, Honoured Guests and fellow Law Society members...'

Necessary opening pleasantries for a formal black tie dinner.

'Last month the United Kingdom's Department of Constitutional Affairs launched a drive to diversify the ethnic, cultural and gender mix in the legal profession.

I am pleased to say the Isle of Man Law Society is fully committed to this initiative.

In selecting me to succeed DD, you replaced a middle age white male from Parliament Street, Ramsey, who likes fast cars and golf with...a middle aged white male from Parliament Street, Ramsey, who likes fast cars and hockey.

I think the Society has come a long way.'

Highly personal and entirely self-created gag works well as a first spike.

'I would however like to lay to rest an unfounded rumour..... the rumour that I have never actually appeared in Court.

Well in fact, I have a one hundred per cent record ... I actually won both of my cases.'

Gentle self-deprecation maintains the laughter.

'Someone who has never had a problem finding his way around any courthouse is XX.

As well as being a top-class Advocate, he is also a top-class cricketer.

There is a lively debate as to who is the best cricketing all rounder of all time: Hadlee, Botham or Imran.

However, there is no doubt that X has been the Island's finest legal all rounder of the last 30 years.

I am delighted to say that his style of advocacy and his style of dress have not changed since 1974.'

Charming use of compliment and gentle insult that illustrates all that is best about the targeted individual.

'Another stalwart of the Manx Bar I intend to pay tribute to tonight is YY.

Y's words in court have always been noted for their detail, their precision...and their sheer quantity.

As an advocate, Y has never lost his will to win.

Mind you, he's caused many Judges to lose their will to live.'

Peter is such a big character that he was worthy of two rather pointed gags. He loved them both.

'ZZ is also a fantastic asset to the council...or so he tells me.

To his credit he has never exploited his vivacious spirit and good looks.

But that has not stopped him trying to.'

None of the personal insult gags are off-the-shelf from a book. They have all been carefully created by exaggerating well-known aspects of the characters in question.

Andrew followed with more personal gags of similar strength, before moving into a more serious section.

Time for his Micro-Statement:

'We are very fortunate to have a Government that does so much to help the businesses and people of the Island..... even though I am concerned about the rising tide of Regulation.'

Now a gag to enhance the Micro-Statement:

'There is a First World War expression 'Don't advance too far in front of your regiment or you will be shot in the arse'.

Sometimes I fear that we advance too far and too fast.'

Key Element 1:

'In the field of tax, I think we've got the balance just right.

And I salute AA for the real vision he has shown over the last decade.

He has managed the almost impossible trick of being trusted and incredibly well respected by both the local and international community.'

Key Element 2:

'However, in some areas of regulation, we are pushing a long way ahead of our competitor jurisdictions.

This has caused a huge amount of secondary legislation.

In 2003 alone, our parliament passed nine hundred pieces of secondary legislation.

In 2004, there will be more than a thousand.

As a small island, we must find simpler ways of protecting our people as well as complying with our international obligations.

Admittedly, different countries have different ways of doing things.

When NASA first put Astronauts into space, they soon discovered that their ballpoint pens wouldn't work in zero gravity.

So they spent the next ten years and 753 million dollars on developing a biro that would write on virtually any surface under virtually any conditions, including total vacuum...

At temperatures ranging from absolute zero ... to over 150 degrees Fahrenheit.

On the other hand, the Russians ... used a pencil.'

Off-the-shelf gag, slightly crow-barred in, but it succeeds in illustrating the essential core of the Key Element.

'The Isle of Man must find its own equivalent of the regulatory pencil!

If we do not, then law will become more and more complicated...and less and less understandable.

And our economy will become less and less competitive.

I am saying all this even though I am hugely optimistic about the future of the Island.

It is precisely because we are so prosperous, that we should so carefully guard our hard-won economic and personal freedoms.'

Key Element 3:

'As the Island has thrived these last 20 years, so has the Society.

And we now number 180 members across 32 firms, employing some 550 people.

I firmly believe that a strong and independent Bar and Judiciary are two of the cornerstones of a strong and independent Isle of Man.

During my time in office, I have had many revelations.

In fact over the past two years I have seen more lights on the road to Damascus than a Lebanese long-distance lorry driver.

One of the most important things that I've learned is the absolutely vital role that legal aid practitioners perform in our Society and also society as a whole.

I would now like to pay tribute to the work of two people who are at the very core of the functioning of the Society.

Firstly, a special thank you to B who organized this evening with her usual thoroughness and good humour. Secondly, I must also congratulate C who commences her maternity leave shortly.

After successfully dealing with 180 lawyers, I'm sure that looking after just one baby will be no problem.'

Andrew even makes pleasantries entertaining.

'Our second speaker this evening is John Dolan.

John is a well-known international speaker, who certainly does not want his identity concealed!

He is an American, but we must try not to hold that against him.'

Back to some really strong personal gags for big laughs just before the End Spike, which has to be a toast in this instance.

'Whether they are from London, Los Angeles or Laxey... Ladies and Gentlemen, the toast is ... Our Guests'.

By the time he sat down, the audience knew that he was a surprisingly entertaining bloke as well as a statesmanlike society president.

The key factors in his overall success were:

- His adherence to the pipeline to create a Micro-Statement and Key Elements.

- Sensitive use of audience knowledge to create personalized gags.

- Long, hard practice in advance and on the day at the venue.

You may not have the sheer determination that Andrew showed ... but he achieved a standard that you should certainly aspire to.

Time Limit

Andrew was so good that I am sure that he terrified the professional After Dinner speakers who were on next. The reason I can be so certain of this is because one of them was *me*. In fact, he managed to get the audience to respond so well, that he got away with breaking a core rule of After Dinner speaking:

Plan to speak for a specific length of time and make damn sure you don't go over it.

You *can* speak for a shorter period of time than planned. In fact, you certainly *should* do if certain things happen (which we will deal with in a moment). Imagine that the audience are silently chanting to themselves:

'What do we want? LAUGHS!'

'How long do we want them for? NOT VERY!'

Never go on for longer. Do not allow yourself to be so intoxicated with your own brilliance that you start to improvise new material on your feet. This is the territory of

Robin Williams and Billy Connolly, not to be trespassed on by a partner in KPMG.

To be fair, Andrew did not make this mistake (nor is he a partner in KPMG). We had planned (and rehearsed) the speech so that it would last for 10 minutes. This is absolutely the upper limit for this sort of speech.

However, he was sometimes getting so much laughter and applause after each gag that he sometimes had to wait 20–30 seconds before continuing. This meant that the speech lasted over 14 minutes.

You may be thinking, 'that's no problem – the audience were clearly loving it'. It is certainly the best problem to have. But there was a danger that he would tire the audience out. Their capacity for enjoyment was stretched to the limit.

Gathering Material

A dinner does not have the same relaxed atmosphere as the pub where you told your mates the one about the lawyer, the Scotsman and the donkey. So, don't use a gag unless you are absolutely certain that:

(a) it is very funny;

(b) it is still funny when *you* tell it.

Carry out a brutal audit of all the funnies you know. Write them out in full. Read them with a cynical eye to yourself.

Are they *really* funny?

If you are really honest with yourself, you will realize that less than 20% of them are. Maybe you are a real wag and 30% of your favourite jokes are up to it. If you are not sure that the gag is funny enough, then it definitely *isn't*.

I am wary of suggesting that you try out these gags on friends. A gag in a conversation with one person is a very different creature to exactly the same words used in front of 100 people.

But some form of sounding board is very helpful. The only people who can give a qualified opinion are people who have some experience of this type of speaking. They are likely to have an instinctive feel for the strength of a gag. If you know that you don't have access to this level of considered opinion, think twice about actually doing the speech. In fact, think eight times.

So you have now trawled through your memory and (I hope) successfully tested some material on vulnerable friends. You have probably come to the conclusion that you have two or three usable stories in the armoury.

Stories are not enough on their own. The most effective After Dinner Speeches are a refined blend of all the different types of material mentioned in Chapter 12.

Lifesavers

Here are some final life-saving tips that will help to give your performance a professional edge:

1. Rehearse the gags so often that you are almost bored with them. Only then can you be confident that you won't fluff them under pressure.

2. There is a fine line between an audience member thinking, 'I'm really looking forward to the speeches,' and him thinking, 'Stuff the speeches, I'm off to the bar'. This line is crossed at around about 10.30pm. Do your very best to make sure that the host/organizer gets you on before then, even if you have to resort to begging and/or threats of violence.

3. Ensure that there is a comfort break before the speeches start. The most receptive After Dinner audience is one with a full stomach but an empty bladder.

4. Insist that someone introduces you. It doesn't have to have the lengthy formality that might be appropriate in a daytime business setting. But you need someone

(the Chairman/Host/Toastmaster) to get the audience quiet. The words might be as simple as:

'Ladies and Gentlemen ... please welcome ... Henry Kissinger.'

5. Drink no alcohol at the dinner. If you are the only totally sober person there, you will have an edge on everyone else.

6. Get to the venue early enough to check that the microphone works. If the organizer says to you 'Don't worry about that, the hotel sound system has worked perfectly for years' – then you should start to panic.

7. Politely insist that every single waiter has left the room *before* you are introduced. Make sure that they are told not to come in again until after you have finished. This means that your best punch line will not be interrupted by 'Who was it that wanted the Drambuie Shandy?'

8. No matter how well the speech is going, resist the urge to ad-lib. The speech is going well because you have *prepared* well, not because you are an innately hilarious bloke. Stick to the script.

9. Prepare a driver's airbag – something that you can rely on in the event of disaster. Sometimes you will be on your feet and you will know from looking at the slumped semi-conscious bodies in front of you that you will have to cut your speech short. Ensure that you have written an emergency sit-down line, which consists of a short but gracious thanks to the host for hospitality shown. This is one of the very few times when pleasantries are useful.

10. Short is best. One of the most successful After Dinner Speeches in history was given by John Pullin, who was then captain of the England rugby union team. The dinner in question was held after the Ireland v. England match at Lansdowne Road, Dublin in 1973. The English

had travelled over to play the match, despite several highly specific terrorist threats. The audience knew that it was an enormous achievement just to be there. When it was his turn to speak, Pullin opened (and *closed*) with the words:

> 'Ladies and Gentlemen, it's great to be here.
>
> We may not be the best team in the world, but at least we turned up.
>
> Goodnight.'

The ensuing standing ovation lasted for five minutes. It is always a good result when the applause lasts for 30 times longer than your speech.

And Finally...

If you do two successful After Dinner Speeches within a short period of time, you will actually start to enjoy the experience. But never forget to feel the pressure. Don't relax so much that the adrenalin stops flowing.

I have certainly never had that problem. I was once the guest speaker at the British Round Table Annual Conference Dinner, which has 1400 guests. The National President introduced me with the following words:

> 'Now it's time for me to bring on our Guest of Honour, Graham Davies.
>
> You may all remember that last year's speaker performed for nearly an hour, which included two encores and three standing ovations. He then donated his fee to charity and bought us all champagne in the bar afterwards.
>
> With all that in mind, we are certainly looking forward to hearing YOU speak, Graham'

Which brings me to the three cardinal rules of After Dinner Speaking:

The first rule is:

Always leave your audience wanting more ...

Chapter 14

SHOULD YOU ACCEPT THE INVITATION?

This is what an over-keen executive in your PR department might whisper in your ear:

'If you are invited to speak at a large event, never ever think of refusing. This is a test of manhood (especially for women). Don't consider whether someone else in your team would be better suited for the occasion. You can always bluff your way through a lack of knowledge.'

Well, don't allow yourself to be wrongly seduced by this sort of inappropriately gung-ho advice.

Speaking at a public conference (or the internal conference of a supplier/client company) can be an extremely effective form of corporate and personal marketing ... *but only if you are a first-class presenter.* In fact, your professional competence will be seen as directly proportional to your presentation skills. Unfair, but that's the way it is.

If you are asked to present at a public event then you must first answer these hard, Bare Knuckle questions:

- Are you really a good enough presenter to represent your company at a public event?

- Would someone else be a better choice?
- Is there a danger that your presentation will actually harm the company's image?
- Is there a danger that your presentation will actually harm your own image?
- Do you really have enough time to prepare and rehearse your presentation?

Only appear at a public conference if you are sure you are up to it. But there is also this brutal question:

'Is this the right event for me to speak at?'

Conference organizers are an innately over-optimistic breed. This has often led to the creation of events which cater for their own interests rather than market demand. The attendance is accordingly pitiful. To help you make the decision about your company's involvement, you must first of all find out about the possible attendees.

Most conference speakers are approached well before an event is advertised. As a result, there are no definite attendees available to speak to. But you can go out and talk to some of the potential attendees that would be targeted by the event organizers. This is your reality check. You can make sure that the proposed content of the conference and your speech is both relevant and appropriate. Vast numbers of specialist conferences have failed because the organizer has not carried out their own reality check.

You should avoid speaking at a public conference as a result of ego, only to find that your time spent preparing has been wasted.

Once you have made the decision that you should speak, there are other factors that you must sort out. After all, you are the one who might end up looking daft.

Assess the Invitation

The organizer's invitation usually goes something like this 'We have divided the morning into 45-minute hour slots (or worse, one hour slots) and we would like you to take one slot on your specialist subject of xxxxx'.

Beware of allowing yourself to be pushed into speaking for a length of time that someone other than you has chosen. It is your assessment of the nature of the content and the needs of the audience that should define the presentation length. This may eventually mean that you have to politely suggest that your presentation lasts a different length of time to that originally envisaged.

These are the vital questions you must ask:

- What is the audience's level of expertise on the topic?
- Is there anyone else speaking on that topic at the same event?
- What does the audience need to know from me about the topic?
- What would the organizer like the Finishing Position of the presentation to be?

Asking the last question may involve you in explaining some Bare Knuckle concepts to your contact. Naturally, I feel that this is a good thing.

When you've got this information (you may have to check it with a second source) you can decide how long you need to speak for to get your distinctive Micro-Statement across. You may feel that this is all overly cautious. It isn't. Clinical calculation ensures that you will never run out of material in front of 500 people when you know that the programme says you are going to speak for another 20 minutes.

Length

If you agree to speak for a particular length of time, religiously stick to that time. Over-running is the mark of the inconsiderate amateur.

Be assertively insistent about how much time you want to speak for. A concise and compelling 20 minutes is far better than a padded-out 45 minutes.

Slides

Don't worry. I am not going to repeat my previous rant. However, here is some Bare Knuckle advice that is particularly true for public events:

The presenters who stand out in the most positive and distinctive way are the ones who use the fewest slides.

This is because industry conferences are usually slide-reading festivals. If you are using Bare Knuckle techniques to create and deliver your presentation, you are certain to rouse the audiences from their slide-ware sleepiness. You may the only presenter who moves away from the lectern and genuinely engages with them instead of the screen.

The Handout Problem

Conference organizers usually insist that their speakers send them a slide-pack well before the day of the event … sometimes weeks in advance. Of course, this encourages the traditional practice of preparing the slides first, with the spoken word being an afterthought.

On arrival, attendees are given a thick file, which contains paper versions of every slide from every presentation that they are going to sit through. This means that they can write notes next to a given slide while the presenter is reading the bullet points on the slide. Exciting, eh?

Of course, there is literally no chance of any slide having any visual impact, because every audience member will see every slide before it appears on the screen.

I have several clients in the investment-banking sector who attend between 15 and 30 of these events a year. They all take the handout files back to the office and put them into a cupboard … until it's time for the once-a-year clear-out. The files then end up in the shredder, without ever having been referred to during their entire residence period within the building.

If you are a Bare Knuckle presenter who uses very few slides and only creates them very late in the preparation process, you will not be able to abide by this strange business convention.

When you receive the organizer's rigid request for your slides, this is what you should do:

1. Politely explain that you will be creating a bespoke presentation for them that will involve the use of very few slides and you would prefer that those slides are seen for the first time when you show them on screen. This will either intrigue or horrify your contact.

2. If they still insist on receiving something in advance, send them a few slides that vaguely relate to your topic, merely to placate them.

3. On the day, early on in your presentation, explain to the audience that you will *not* be using those slides because you have been working on your content over the previous few days to make it as up-to-date as possible (which will be true, I hope).

I am sure that the above sequence will have made you cringe a little. It certainly ought to, as step 2 is arguably misleading. Nevertheless, the combined effect is that you will achieve the best presentational result for the organizers, the audience and yourself.

Your Introduction

The topic of Introductions is dealt with in more detail in Chapter 15. But here are a few pointers about how to deal with the issue at a public event.

When speaking After Dinner or at a business conference, an introduction by a third party can greatly assist the speaker to achieve a vertical takeoff. However, it has to be exactly the *right* introduction.

The introduction must support your credibility and assist in positioning your experience and topic relative to the day's proceedings.

The only way of making certain that it is done correctly is to write it yourself and rehearse the introduction with the presenter involved.

In my experience, the person doing the introductions must be watched carefully. There is often an overwhelming desire in the introducer to strut their speaking prowess. The result is a long, boring and inappropriate introduction that makes you angry. You must type it out for them and explain how badly your self-esteem will be dented if they don't stick to the script.

Music

Despite the qualms I expressed in Chapter 10, in front of an audience of several hundred people, walk-up music can add to the overall effectiveness of your introduction. However, remember that:

- Inappropriately over-the-top music can generate disbelief, scorn or even laughter. If you were an audience member, how would you react if a speech on corporate debt recovery was immediately preceded by *Eye of the Tiger?*
- If the speaker does not have far to travel from seat to stage, the music will not have time to take hold and the short playing time will look amateurish.

What slot?

Badly constructed conferences have speaker after speaker with no change or let-up. You may not have a chance to dictate when in the day you will be speaking, but if you do have a choice, the pole speaking position is the first slot after the morning coffee break. You will be remote from the housekeeping issues that would inevitably be presented at the beginning of the day. If the speakers in the first half of the morning were good, they will be an excellent warm-up act for you. If they were not so good, then the audience will have had a coffee break to regain their optimism.

The first half of the morning is too early and the audience will be too cold. In the later stages of the morning, audiences will have a tendency to fantasise about other things, such as lunch. Immediately after lunch, there is the highly unsought-after graveyard shift. At public conferences, speakers in this slot will be subjected to audience members arriving late talking and lapsing into semi-consciousness.

After tea in the afternoon it is often a struggle for audiences to maintain coherent thought, focus and consciousness.

The content of a conference should demonstrate a logical sequence that you should fit into. Never assume that the organizer is sensible enough to know this. Make sure that you receive *in writing* a list of all other potential speakers (plus their phone numbers and e-mail addresses). Do not rely on a casual phone conversation. You have to be ruthless in looking after your own interests as a speaker. This means that you must be absolutely certain that you are not following a speaker who may be using largely the same material as you.

Ensure that you talk *directly* to the other potential speakers. Don't rely on a hearsay account of what they *might* say.

Integrating links to past and future speakers at the event will make you look organized, generous and sympathetic to the overall theme. You will avoid repetition or accidental contradictions. After all, the most important thing is making sure that *you* look good.

If you ever get to the level where you are good enough to be paid fees for your speaking, then I heartily recommend that you join the Professional Speaking Association. It is an organization that utterly believes in free speech, but not free speeches. You will learn all about the business of speaking: how to get money from where your mouth was. I am not sure whether the previous sentence makes sense, but I still like it.

CHAPTER 15

CHALLENGING BUSINESS SITUATIONS

By the time you read this chapter, I hope you have had the chance to use the Bare Knuckle method several times in formal, stand-up presentations. This chapter will show you how you can adapt what I trust has become *your* standard technique to a wide variety of different situations.

There are two reasons why the situations covered in this chapter cause so much anguish, even to experienced presenters:

- They occur relatively infrequently.
- People often go into them without a specific toolbox of techniques.

Naturally, I am confident that you will find that the Bare Knuckle methodology can be adapted triumphantly for each of them, whether you are in a boardroom, ballroom or broadcast studio.

Remember the key pieces of the Bare Knuckle Preparation Pipeline:

Knockout Result

Audience Analysis

Starting Position

Finishing Position

Micro-Statement

Brainstorming

Filtering

Key Elements

Spikes

The applicability of each of these concepts varies widely for each situation, but the overall methodology should still be a constant source of comfort to you, no matter what the circumstances.

Introducing Another Speaker

Nearly every speaking situation requires some form of introduction. The one exception is where the audience is very small (two or less). The introducer and the speaker being introduced should prepare introductions jointly. This section contains advice for people in *both* roles.

An introduction should have a Starting Position and a Finishing Position, just like any other presentation. The Micro-Statement of any introduction should be the answer to the question:

'Why should we listen to this person that is about to start speaking in a minute?'

Key Elements might include

- the presenter's academic qualifications;
- their business experience;
- their history with that company;
- an indication of why they are capable of speaking about the topic at hand;
- their *name*.

When you are the speaker being introduced, it always pays to be paranoid. You may not be able to choose the person who introduces you (e.g. if it has to be your boss, your client contact or the Chairman of the relevant association).

However, you can – politely but firmly – tell them exactly what you want them to say. You must keep control of this. It is not good enough to just have a quick chat with the introducer, hand him your CV and expect him to choose the best words. *You have to make the choice for them.*

You need an introduction to satisfy both yourself and the audience. The audience needs to know that their time is not going to be wasted – and they need to know this even before you open your mouth. A certain level of interest should be stimulated which will make them receptive to your First Spike. But satisfying your own needs is just as important. A good introduction means that you will feel you are set up for success. Psychologically, you are running at full pace before you hit the ground.

The best introductions are short and blunt (like all the best presentations). Introducers do not write the best introductions. The speakers that they are introducing *do.*

Some examples:

John Smith is a consultant who has been hired by Carnage Computers to improve an indifferent sales performance. After some discussions with senior management, the sales force has been brought together to hear his preliminary conclusions about what the next step should be. This is how the Sales Director might introduce him:

'Our sales have dropped by 40%t over the last six months. We cannot allow this to continue. I have decided that this is too big a problem to solve without seeking the best possible advice. That is why I have hired John Smith.

John is a Stamford MBA who spent four years with McKinsey before moving to join the sales team at Pineapple Computers. After five years he was appointed VP for Sales Worldwide. During his time in that position, Pineapple's sales grew by 180%.

In 1995 he left Pineapple to set up his own consultancy "Sales Momentum". Their unique approach has already produced impressive results for IBM, Ford and Prudential.

Over the next six months, he will be working very closely with you to help us back to the level of success that we need.

Ladies and Gentlemen – please welcome JOHN SMITH'.

Notice the inclusion of the key elements:

- qualifications;
- history with McKinsey and IBM;
- relevant sales achievements;
- the fact that he is going to be working closely with his audience.

Everyone in that room now knows that they need to listen to him.

On the other hand, here is an introduction I might like to be used when I am introduced as the After Dinner Speaker at a large, formal event:

'After a lot of thought, we decided that our guest speaker this evening should be morally sound, compassionate ... and, above all ... cheap.

And so we have invited a lawyer.

His speaking style has been described as a cross between Voltaire and the Sunday Sport.

During his career at the Criminal Bar, Graham tells me that Jeffrey Archer, George Michael and Conrad Black are just three of the people who were extremely grateful that he's never represented them.'

Clearly, this introduction is designed at least to make the audience smile, if not laugh out loud. It should at least prepare them for the fact that the bloke being introduced is probably quite amusing.

But notice the key elements. The audience is being told that

- I am a Barrister;
- doing criminal work;
- and unlikely to be serious.

Also notice the underlines that show which words I want the introducer to emphasize. I have these words printed on a plastic card in idiot-proof size print. I politely insist on the introducer rehearsing the introduction in front of me. I also insist on two further things:

- that they use the introduction verbatim, with no alterations;
- that they do *not* say 'this is an introduction that Graham has insisted that I read out verbatim ...'

Many inexperienced introducers do not understand that this simply murders any chance of getting laughs.

Sitting Down To Present

It is much more difficult to present in a compelling way when sitting down as opposed to when you are standing up. The very act of standing conveys a certain amount of authority. This probably goes back to our schooldays when we spent 12 years or sitting and listening to people who supposedly knew more than we did at the time.

However, if there are four people or less in front of you, standing up to present to them feels, well ... *strange.* The process of communication ceases to be natural.

As a result of many years of both stand-up and sit-down presentation, I feel that five people is the minimum critical mass for a stand-up performance. In fact, I firmly believe that you definitely *should* stand up if you have 5 or more people in front of you ... unless there are specific circumstances that prevent you from doing so.

For instance, it may just be a rigid convention within your company or industry that everyone stays seated during board gatherings, pitches or other types of meeting. Even if you are fully imbued with a Bare Knuckle attitude, I do not suggest that you break with an unspoken rule like this that has probably been in place for some time. A decision to stand up may come across as inappropriately arrogant rather than distinctively assertive.

Many of the situations covered in this chapter will probably involve presenting from a seated position.

Seating Arrangements

Eye-lines are particularly crucial in a sit-down situation. I recommend that you take the risk of politely arranging people where you want them, especially if they are an important client or senior to you in your own organisation. You need to be facing the crucial individuals … even if it means asking whether you or they can move. It is very difficult to persuade someone when you have to painfully twist your neck to look them in the eye.

Delivery When Seated

Here is the key ingredient for presenting with impact when seated:

Convince yourself that you are standing up, even though your buttocks are supporting you rather than your feet.

This mindset will allow you to generate stand-up authority from a sit-down position. You should aim to:

- Speak with the dinner-party intensity of engagement as described in Chapter 9.

- Make sure that the volume of your voice is 5% louder than in casual conversation.

- Sit upright to ensure that your height is maximized.

- Swivel your head around as much as possible so that you are engaging the people sitting next to you as much as the people sitting in front of you.

- Have your hands loosely in front of you on the table, so that they are available to move with the flow of what you are saying.

These techniques will give you a sharp edge on anyone else in that room, without making you stand out in a way that is harmful.

Team Presentations

Team presentations are unwieldy beasts. They can quickly lurch out of control unless your content preparation and rehearsal adhere to a strict process.

I use the phrase 'team presentation' to refer to a situation where there are two or more presenters who are speaking together to achieve a common purpose. For instance, a senior executive, a sales person and a specialist individual fund manager may act as the pitch team when their organization is attempting to persuade a pension fund to use their services.

The main problem that the pitch team have is that they have a great deal of information that they could include, but simply not enough presentational time available. They will be allocated a 30-minute slot on a day where the target company is seeing seven other similar organizations.

It is vital that each individual understands and focuses on their specific role, while at the same time never losing sight of the overall desired finishing position. The best way of doing this is to adopt a rigid sequence of events that uses the Bare Knuckle method at every stage. Using the fund management example above, here is what should happen:

1. Appoint a leader. The most senior executive is the obvious choice in this example, even though they will probably be the member of the team who will spend the shortest amount of time actually presenting on the day. The most formal part of their role will probably to give a general introduction, so they may well be using material that they can pick up off their personal presentational shelf. There are only so many ways that the organization can be described at the beginning of a pitch of this type, so they should have honed his standard remarks on previous occasions.

The leader's main job is to co-ordinate the preparation of content, the logistics of the venue and the overall performance on the day. At every stage, they must maintain an accurate overview of what has been done and what still needs to be done.

2. Brainstorm. Whoever does make it to the brainstorming meeting should carry out a thorough assessment of the latest information available about the target client. They should use this to go through an Audience Analysis, which will be very brief: it is highly likely that the pension fund trustees are people with management experience, but without any specialist financial expertise.

The desired Finishing Position will be easy to decide: at the end of the presentation, they want the audience to decide that their organization is the best choice to manage their funds.

The Finishing Position that each of the presenters will have for the audience of pension fund trustees can be defined as follows:

Team Leader: that the audience have a clear idea of their organization's place and status in the market.

Sales Executive: that the audience feel that the organization has the correct infrastructure to support their needs.

Fund Management Specialist: that their team are extremely well qualified to invest the client's money in the Asian market.

By the end of this initial meeting, all the players should have agreed on the respective Micro-Statements for their own individual pieces.

3. Write it. The players should now create their Baseline Texts and e-mail them to each other for comments and mutual approval. The word 'create' is probably not really accurate in this context. Each player will probably have prepared previously a relatively standard presentation that can be tailored and tweaked according to the characteristics of a given target client.

I would certainly encourage this practice. Even though I am an advocate of intense tailoring of presentations to fit the needs of the audience, I agree that there is enormous value in using large chunks of carefully calculated material that has been honed in battle before.

4. Team rehearsal. All the players should force themselves to rehearse in front of each other, even if this feels awkward and seems to take up time that they would prefer to do other things.

I once asked the main pitching team how much rehearsal they did before a pitch and their leader said, 'Well, it depends on how long the taxi journey to the client is'.

I suggest that an hour of rehearsal is a reasonable investment of time when trying to attract several million pounds worth of business. Each player gets the chance to make sure that what they say dovetails appropriately with the words of their colleagues.

5. On the day. During the actual performance on the day, each team member has to remember that they are on show at all times, even when they are not speaking. While one team member is speaking, his colleagues must ensure that they are seen to be paying attention, rather than wandering off into their own world. Ideally, they should look as fascinated as they would like their target audience to be.

The Team Leader should act as a link between the audience and the rest of the team. They are the member of the team who should be the most sensitive to audience reaction as the presentations progress. They should have a good enough knowledge of the content of each individual presentation so that they can immediately, and openly, suggest a change in direction if necessary. The Leader can also be the one who decides which team member answers particular questions as they arise.

Answering Questions....again!

To various different extents, the remaining situations in this chapter all involve answering questions. Most people are far too relaxed in their attitude to this. Even experienced and accomplished corporate performers who always prepare thoroughly for formal presentations are likely to walk into Q & A. This can lead to the positive effect of lovingly crafted and punchily delivered set-piece presentation being horribly diminished by a couple of ill-judged responses to relatively innocuous queries.

Nearly every conversation you ever have will involve answering questions. I am not suggesting that you need a Bare Knuckle attitude when a friend asks you the time or your spouse enquires about the day you have just had. These are *casual* situations. I merely want to give you the weaponry to be more robust in *pressure* situations.

A pressure situation is where the answer to each question can have a significant effect on an important overall result you are trying to achieve.

For instance:

- At the end of a formal presentation (as covered in Chapter 10).
- When you have submitted a written proposal and the recipient needs to clarify issues arising from it.
- On-stage interviews.
- Panel discussions.
- Media interviews.

The above is not meant to be an exhaustive list. I am certain that a few moments' thought will remind you of several occasions where you cringe at the memory of an unsatisfactory response by yourself or someone else. Here is a list of typical problems that clients have told me about:

- 'I know my subject really well, but I just can't get the first words out of my mouth.'
- 'I try to say too much and I can see everyone's eyes glazing over.'
- 'I think I answer pretty well but I just don't know how to stop.'

Using a combination of the Preparation Pipeline (see page 263), and the FIR, SSS and Pause-Spike formulae in Chapter 11 can conquer all these problems.

On-stage Interviews

On-stage conference interviews are a cop-out. Executives like them because they think they don't need to prepare. Organizers like them because they satisfy the fad for interaction rather than formal presentation. I accept that conferences that consist of a stream of talking-heads-supporting-slides are extremely boring. However, unless it is done well, an interview on stage can take audience ennui to a new high.

The problem is that conversations are just not designed to occur in front of other people. In a casual one-to-one conversation, each participant crafts his words just for the other individual ... and rightly so.

If you are going to be interviewed in front of any audience, you must remember at all times that *it is not a chat, it is a performance.* This advice is also valid for radio and television audiences.

Under the next two headings, I will discuss how to prepare for two typical scenarios, before going on to deal with delivery issues that are common to both.

Pre-prepared

The most likely reason for you being interviewed on stage is because you have a particular area of knowledge or expertise that someone has deemed is necessary listening for their conference audience. That audience might consist of colleagues in your own company or a more diverse group at an industry event.

You will probably be told that you will have a certain amount of time on stage (probably no more than 15 minutes). You will probably be working with a professional interviewer, who might be a TV presenter or specialist conference facilitator. The professional will have been given a brief about you and your knowledge base.

Even though the other person will have more experience of this situation, you should still **grab as much control as you can**.

Go through a Preparation Pipeline as though you were preparing a formal presentation, but once you have decided on your Key Elements, don't bother writing out a Baseline Text. Instead, just draft a few core phrases.

Then, phone the interviewer and tell them your list of Key Elements, firmly suggesting that they form the bones of the interview. The professional will be delighted, because you have done a lot of their work for them. Believe me, they won't be in the slightest bit offended. I have performed the interviewing role at dozens of events and only a tiny number of the people I have worked with on stage have been this presentationally pro-active. And they were always the ones that really shone on the day.

Depending on the rapport that you build up with the interviewer, you could even go as far as suggesting the exact wording of potential questions. This approach runs the risk of removing the spontaneity from the interview. But I don't care. Spontaneity is over-rated.

There will probably be some time allocated for on-site rehearsal of the interview. Just make sure that you rehearse sounding spontaneous. Listen carefully to any coaching that the interviewer gives you during the rehearsal phase. It is in their interests to make you look good.

Not so pre-prepared

You may be someone who is bold enough to thrust themselves into a public interview that is not rehearsed in any way. This may be because you are a politician or a particularly confident senior executive. Or the sadistic organiser just thinks that it would be super fun not to give you any notice of the questions.

Nevertheless, you will still know the topic you are going to be asked about, so you must go through the Pipeline as before. You must ensure that you have some pithy, pre-prepared phrases about the likely topics. Remember to prepare for both difficult and easy questions (see Chapter 10), bearing in mind that it is sometimes the easy ones that generate the daftest answers.

Delivery on stage

You are likely to be seated when on stage. The equipment provided for this purpose is often comically unsuitable:

The comfy sofa is designed to discourage you from sitting upright. Your buttocks are likely to end up lower than your knees.

The school cafeteria chair is the mark of a very low-budget event, that you should be ashamed to be part of. This sort of chair is upright, unattractive and almost impossible to feel comfortable on. And it is usually orange.

The bar stool is something on which it almost impossible to maintain either balance or dignity, especially if you are wearing a skirt.

The James Bond villain swivel chair is probably the most pleasant and effective option, but beware of the ease with which you can turn into a helicopter.

Whatever seating device you are provided with it is likely to be placed at an angle to the front of the stage, i.e. not facing straight at the audience. The interviewer will either sit in an identical chair a few feet away or stand in roughly the same area.

Sit upright, with the bottom of your spine lightly touching the back of the chair. I do not mean rigidly upright, but leaning just slightly forward towards the interviewer. Place you hand loosely in your lap, touching but not holding each other. Don't cross your legs. You will find that the most comfortable position for your feet is to have one slightly in front of the other, as though you were just about to get up.

At all times, you should pretend to yourself that you are standing up, as though the chair were there by a strange accident. This mindset will help you to perform instead of just chat.

As you listen and respond to the interviewer's questions, think FIR or SSS as described in Chapter 11. As you deliver the first sentence of your first answer, look straight back into the eyes of the interviewer, as you would in normal conversation. Then you must carry out an extremely unnatural presentation manoeuvre ... something that is the key to success in an on-stage interview:

Break eye contact with the interviewer and turn your head and body so that you are now talking straight to the audience.

Do not keep your head in just one position. Swivel your head around so that you are making a sweep of eye contact with various sections of the audience in the same way as you would in a stand-up presentation. Remember that the interviewer is also an audience member so he has to be included in the sweep.

When you are delivering your last sentence, make sure that your final sweep finishes with you looking back at the interviewer, so that you end up where you started.

This technique will feel very awkward and actually rather rude when you first try it. But it is the only way of making sure that the whole audience can be drawn into what other wise could be a piece of one-to-one conversation that excludes them.

Panel Discussions

These are becoming more and more common in both business and political conferences. They fit in with the current trend for this sort of event to be as interactive as possible, rather than merely a sequence of monologues.

Typically, a panel discussion will involve three or four people sitting behind a table, with a moderator either standing or seated on another part of the stage. The moderator will bring up a topic and ask each panellist in turn for their views.

Sadly, this is usually a recipe for tedium. There is a tendency for panellists to speak in an un-focused ramble. And the format is likely to lead to too much *agreement*. Instead of getting a lively debate, you are more likely to hear panellists say:

'Of course, I agree with John and let me re-iterate something he has already said....'

This sort of bland attitude is never going to be compelling.

Another problem is that the participants see panel participation as a more attractive option than doing a formal presentation because they don't think they have to prepare much, or indeed at all.

If you want to make a Bare Knuckle impact when you appear on a panel, follow this formula: Control, Differentiate, Deliver.

Take control by deciding the sort of questions that you really should be asked about your areas of expertise ... the obvious and the not-so-obvious, as well as the easy and difficult. Enlist the help of well informed colleagues for this.

Make contact in advance of the event with the moderator and suggest these as areas of enquiry. Find out what other areas they are likely to be interested in. The moderator will be delighted that you are being so pro-active.

They should be even more delighted when you make an effort to *differentiate yourself*. Find out from the moderator and directly from other panellists what their views are likely to be on 'your' topic...and get a broad idea of the views they are likely to express on 'their' topic.

Then make sure that what you are likely to say is different.

Deliver by using a combination of the FIR, SSS or Pause/Spike formulae detailed in Chapter 11. There may be a particular sub-topic that (just in case), you deem to be so important and so likely to be a core target of audience interest that you decide to create full presentation, with Spikes, Key Elements and a Micro-Statement. Although even then you should make sure that you are never speaking for longer than 90 seconds.

I am not suggesting that you be annoyingly contrarian for the sake of it. But you should be able to make yourself and your opinions stand out in such a way that it benefits both your audience and your reputation.

Media Interviews

Although I have been interviewed many times on TV and radio, I do not hold myself out as an expert on this genre. Media interviews are still an arena where I am a learner rather than a teacher. I just want to share with you the most important things I have learned by experience.

1. **Never relax.** Unless you are a public figure of some magnitude, the interview will last less than four minutes, and consist of only three or four questions.

2. **Prepare two or three killer phrases** in advance about your topic: phrases that you know are striking enough for a viewer or listener to tell other people about. Be determined to get one or two of these phrases into one of your answers, no matter what.

3. **Work out a Micro-Statement** that you will almost definitely include in your first answer, just in case the interview is cut short for reasons beyond your control. Remember, the first question will always be the one that gives you the most latitude.

4. **Be particularly pointed in the way that you nail the Closing Spike** for each answer. This conveys sharp authority on both radio and television.

5. **Smile a bit more than you think you should.** When you are psyched up to perform fast and hard in a

three-minute slot, it is far too easy to scowl with your face and your voice, unless you make a specific effort *not* to.

The topic of media interviews is covered superbly in *The Pocket Media Coach* by Alan Stevens (How to Books, 2005).

Telephone Conferences

There are two types of telephone conference. The first is where only one person is on the other end of the line and the second is where there are two or more at the end of the line.

The most distinctive aspect of both types of call, compared to all the other situations we have discussed so far, is that you cannot see your audience! This is both an advantage and a disadvantage.

It's an advantage because you can spread out a huge array of notes in front of you and also refer to information on a computer screen without worrying about this getting in the way of human to human engagement. The big disadvantage is that you are unable to use eye contact to gauge how well your words are being received.

One-to-One Phone Conferences

When does a mere phone-call become a phone conference? In my view the answer is: when the result of the call is important enough for you to need to prepare for it.

This is one of the few situations where your Opening Spike could usefully be an attempt to set the agenda:

> *'What I would like to do in this call is to explore exactly where you feel your current training provider does not quite fit your needs and I then I'd like to tell you a bit about how my consultancy works.'*

As the phone call develops, you should attempt to take extensive notes of what the other person is saying. This is easier if you are using a hands-free device. This will help you to keep track of exactly what has been covered and may also give you the chance to quote back to the other person their exact words later on in the call ... as long as you do this in a helpful and positive way rather than in a tone which is sounding like you are trying to catch them out!

As the conversation develops, and you feel that you have collected enough information about their current situation there will come a time when you sense that it is right to use your Micro-Statement. One that I have used several times to describe the activities of my own consultancy is as follows:

'I am confident that we have a client list, track record and methodology that is better than anyone else who works in the Fund Management sector.'

Of course, you may decide that you do not want to use this highly potent weapon during this particular call, because you have come to the conclusion that the time is just not right. You may decide that you would like to spend more time observing the information the other person has given you to create a more tailored Micro-Statement for a later phone call, follow-up document or face-to-face meeting.

Your End Spike can still be used before the final farewell pleasantries, and should consist of a statement of what you believe the next step should be:

'I will send you a two-page document within 48 hours which will set out a brief plan of our proposed intervention, together with a note of the costs involved.'

These are the sort of words that give the other person confidence that there will be specific and valuable result that arises from the call.

Group Phone Conferences

Group phone conferences inevitably involve an element of predatory competition. You have to be prepared to fight hard and fast in the relatively short time slot that will be available for you to speak.

In the banking sector, there are often phone conferences with 20 or more participants. Each person phones into a central number and an individual from the host bank tries to act as the chairman of the proceedings. There should have been some e-mail contact in advance to ensure that everyone has a grasp of who else is present on the line.

The chairman will probably ask each caller to briefly give their opinion on the issue at hand. Despite the fact that the telephone is an innately interactive piece of technology, group calls create an environment that actually stifles interaction. If a genuine discussion breaks out, it is likely that the call will degenerate into a squabbling babble that no-one can follow.

If you have prepared in a Bare Knuckle way, you will have a distinct advantage over everyone else. They may have scribbled a few notes on a scrap of paper. You will have prepared a Micro-Statement, enhanced by Key Elements and Spikes, with your whole presentation probably condensed into 60 seconds or less.

The most difficult aspect of this situation is its sheer tedium. Most participants will ramble and merely echo what has been already said. You should listen on a hands-free device, so that you can constantly adjust your own likely content. By the time it is your turn to speak, you should feel ferociously keen to get your point across in an assertively professional way. You are highly likely to be the most prepared and focused individual involved in the call….and the most likely to have their words remembered and respected.

Chairing the Call

If you are the host who is chairing the call, you will have to deal with several challenges:

- Ensuring that all the expected participants have turned up and introduced themselves.
- Setting and keeping to an agenda.
- Making a note of what is said and by whom.

You will have to do this at the same time as being mentally available to respond to issues immediately as they arise during the call. To do all this, you need to be superbly organized and have three pairs of hands. The latter requirement can be satisfied by enlisting the help of two other colleagues. One should have the sole task of writing down everything that is said. The other should have the responsibility of ticking off headings on the agenda and steering you along the direction in which the call needs to go.

This will allow you to be the presentational leader who ensures that everyone gets their say within a framework of focused professionalism.

The Last-Minute Request

Imagine your joy when your boss says to you, almost casually, 'I've just had lunch with our worldwide CEO and a couple of his immediate reports. Could you nip up to my office in about quarter of an hour and spend a few minutes telling them what you think is going to happen in Europe over the next year?'.

This is precisely the request that an Investment Banker client of mine once had. Europe was his specialist area of knowledge. His problem was that he had too much information available in his head rather than too little. Fortunately, he had absorbed my coaching and always made sure that he never went to work unarmed: he always carries a few index cards in his jacket pocket. Make sure you follow his example.

He used those cards in the emergency drill below, which allows you to prepare a presentation in 10 minutes:

1. Think carefully about the **audience** you have just been told about. Immediately work out what you would like to say if you only had 10 seconds in which to say it. Do not worry about the difference between this Micro-Message and a Finishing Position. (two minutes)

2. Write the **Micro-Statement** out in full on an index card. You will use this as your **First Spike**. (one minute)

3. On a second card, write down the headings of the first **five things** that spring to mind that support your Micro-Statement. (two minutes)

4. Choose the best three and write them as headings under the Micro-Statement on the first card. These are your **Key Elements**. (two minutes)

5. Think of an **End Spike** that echoes your First Spike without repeating it verbatim … and write it out in brief note form on the bottom of the card. The fact that you have not written it out in full gives you some room for thought and manoeuvre if the words you actually say in the cauldron of relatively spontaneous presentation do not quite come out as neatly as you hope. It is possible that your End Spike may have to be changed on the hoof. (two minutes)

6. Use the time remaining to read through the card, forcing yourself to **elaborate on the Key Elements** in your head. (one minute)

I have allowed five minutes of the suggested schedule for you to get to your boss's office. At the risk of people you walk past thinking that you are somewhat disturbed, try to mutter out loud some of the crucial phrases on the way. This means that three of the most important people in your world will hear at least some words that you have calculated and said before.

Your index card may end up looking like this:

Market will show a great deal of volatility, but we can take advantage.

- Liquidity poor
- USA over-reliance
- Commodity shortage

Difficult conditions, goodish for us, possible profit.

The notes above were used by my client to sustain a five-minute presentation. The emergency drill leaves out all the parts of the Bare Knuckle methodology that involves the use of in-depth thought about a series of questions. Brainstorming is curtailed dramatically and there can be no editing. But it gives you an excellent chance of creating and delivering something that briefly gives the audience what they need as well as enhancing your credibility.

Presenting To The Board

Board meeting agendas are always too packed. It is rare for a board meeting to end at the scheduled time. If you are invited to present to them, it is vital that you get to the point very quickly indeed. Directors are the sort of people who hate to waste time. Therefore, you have to be ready to shorten your performance dramatically if they suddenly indicate that they can give you less time than you were originally told.

And never tell them stuff they already know. A sure way of annoying them is to start your time in front of them with the words, 'Before I tell you our solution, I thought it might be useful to remind you of the background to our problem....'

If you are given a time limit for your presentation in advance of the meeting, stick to it rigidly. In fact, go further than that: make sure that you are definitely under the time limit *and* structure your presentation to allow some scope for you to jettison material instantly.

Let's say you have decided on five key elements. In a boardroom situation, you should certainly plan to present the three most important first. This means that you can dump the last two if you are suddenly put under time pressure.

More assertive board members may demand that you get to your recommendation almost immediately, so you should also be ready to come out with your Micro-Statement at any time. In fact, you should assume that you will be interrupted and challenged constantly, and regard it as a pleasant surprise if you are not.

This all means that the preparation you put into a board presentation has to be particularly ruthless when it comes to editing.

You can only win big if you think small.

Directors have a tendency to challenge assumptions. So make sure that you challenge your own before they get the chance. So look ruthlessly at your Baseline Text and make sure that you *can justify concisely every assertion* that you make.

This tough testing is vital, because a board is an audience where the fight for their attention will be constant.

I could easily have included a couple of dozen business situations in this chapter, but that would have made for a very long book. The ones I have selected should be enough to make you confident that you can adapt the Bare Knuckle method to any business situation where your spoken communication skills are put under pressure. The final step in becoming a Bare Knuckle presenter is discovering how you can be more persuasive in your personal life.

CHAPTER 16

CHALLENGING PERSONAL SITUATIONS

Effective presenting is not something that has to be confined to the workplace. I have chosen a few common non-work scenarios just to give you an idea of how the Bare Knuckle method can help you to be more compelling in a huge variety of circumstances.

The situations in this chapter require a degree of subtlety that is arguably not present in the rest of the book. The fight for the audience's attention is not so intense (e.g. complaining or getting an upgrade) or has already been largely won before you say your first words (weddings and funerals).

I recommend that these are instances where, in the main, your Bare Knuckles should be covered by a velvet glove.

The stories you have read in previous chapters may make you think that I am always a bit of a brute. Well, it's time for you to see my cuddly side.

Wedding Speeches

Here is a sentence that I bet you thought you would never read in this book:

This is a situation where you don't need a Micro-Statement.

I will now refine the apparent blasphemy above: you don't need to *agonize* over a Micro-Statement, as essentially Micro-Statement *and* Finishing Positions in wedding speeches will always be the same. A wedding speaker will always want the audience to enjoy a few laughs while emphasizing what thoroughly nice people the bride and groom are.

But there is definitely a place for Audience Analysis, Brainstorming, Key Elements and Spikes.

No speech of any sort at any wedding should last more than eight minutes. Many brilliantly memorable ones are a great deal shorter.

The Best Man

Even though it is unlikely to be the first speech at a wedding reception, I will discuss the best man's speech first, because it is certainly the most important. At British Christian and Jewish weddings, it is considered to be one of the focal points of the day.

A best man really should feel under pressure. Everybody will be looking forward to his speech. He is expected to be the cabaret turn after all the boring bits are finished. He will have had months to prepare ... so he had better be funny.

Essentially, a best man speech is a highly specialized form of after dinner speech that runs through the career highs and comic lows of the groom's life and reminds the audience what a splendid chap he is. With most wedding audiences, the journey to this Finishing Position should be a short and easy one. If you give them even the slightest excuse to laugh, the audience will encourage you by doing exactly that.

A certain amount of Audience Analysis is still necessary. It would certainly be helpful to know if there is a particular type of person or profession that is heavily represented (lawyers, accountants, policemen). This makes it easier to tailor any humour that you are thinking of using.

The key to success is clever use of the information that is available.

Audience Analysis questions for the Best Man to ask

- What are the full names of the bride and groom?
- How did you get to know them?
- How old are they?
- Has either been married before?
- What are their educational backgrounds?
- What is their professional history?
- Precisely when, where and how did they meet?
- What are the most distinctive characteristics of their personalities?
- Are there any particularly notorious incidents in their respective pasts that might be of use?
- Is there anything distinctive about any of the parents that might be of use to us?
- Are there any other major characters present who might be worthy of mention?
- What striking stories are there about the major characters?
- Are there any taboo subjects which must *not* be mentioned?
- What is the religious persuasion of the event?
- How many speeches will be made at the event?
- Who will they be given by?
- Will you be able to find out the likely content of the other speeches?
- How good are they likely to be?
- How many people will be present?

- What is the audience age range, nationality split and dominant characteristics? e.g. are 60% of them from the same profession or the same school?
- What time of day will it be?
- Will a microphone be available? What type?
- How about a lectern?
- Is there a Toastmaster or MC?
- If not, who will introduce you?

The answers to the questions above will give you a factual foundation on which to build something entertaining.

Many books on speaking advise inexperienced speakers not to try being funny unless it comes naturally.

Here is the bad news: if you are the best man, you have *got to be* funny.

You will find detailed advice on the creation and sourcing of humour in Chapter 12. There are dozens of easily Googlable wedding websites and a few of them do actually contain some useful funny material. However, the most valuable source of humour should be true anecdotes about the groom. Well, *almost* true.

Under no circumstances should the best man refer to the previous sexual history of the bride or groom … either with each other or anyone else. That sort of humour is only funny in movies. The potential comedy upside is greatly outweighed by the potential friendship-ending downside.

Anecdote selection

Use the brainstorming centipede from Chapter 4, perhaps with the input of other friends of the groom and members of his close family. There are bound to be a few spicy stories about even the blandest of future husbands. You hope.

But beware of what I call the 'Best Man Syndrome'. This is the phenomenon where the best man tells an anecdote which he and his mates find very funny, usually because the story involves a few of them as well. Unfortunately, the event recounted is either too obscure or too obscene for anyone but them to relate to. The rest of the audience has to make a real effort even to smile politely.

So ... filter the candidate anecdotes by using the following test question:

'Will at least 80% of the audience find this anecdote amusing?'

Even if you feel that all the anecdotes you have come up with pass the test, I would still advise you to choose no more than three of them in the speech.

Anecdote Editing

The anecdotes chosen will make up your Key Elements, so write them out in full. It is vital that you tell each anecdote in the fewest number of words possible so that you maximize comic impact without trying the patience of the audience. A certain amount of embellishment is to be encouraged and is expected. No-one would want your funny bone to be limited by sticking to just the cold facts.

So ... the balance to be achieved in your anecdotal content is best summed up as follows:

Make them slightly funnier and a lot shorter than real life.

I will illustrate this by showing you the Baseline Text of a best man speech for the wedding of two fictional characters called Kevin and Sharon. In fact, they are an amalgam of the characteristics of several people for whom I have drafted speeches in the past.

The speech is a *skeleton*, rather than a full Baseline Text, but is nevertheless an effective illustration of the balance that you can achieve between truth, embellishment, seriousness and off-the-shelf one-liners from your own comic library.

I have put performance directions in brackets and have inserted my comments.

'Ladies and Gentlemen, on behalf of Sharon, I recently hired a consultancy to carry out some market research about the characteristics of the ideal bridegroom.

And apparently he should be:

charming,

sophisticated ...

and own an Olympic standard clay pigeon shooting range.'

(TURN TO BRIDE)

'Well, Sharon ... one out three isn't too bad.'

Naturally, this line reflects one of the bride's great passionsother than her new husband.

'I am very much aware that mine is the last of five speeches.

The good news is that I never speak in public for any longer than I can make love in private.

So ... in conclusion ...'

'Compared to many people in this room, I've only known Kevin for a relatively few years – so I don't know very much about the appalling depravity of his youth.

Mind you, it would still be very easy for me to slanderously tarnish the memory of this marvellous day ...

So here goes ...'

You would probably add about 90 seconds of factual history.

'Beneath the hard exterior, there lies a soft, cuddly romantic.

I am sure that it was this spirit of innocent romance that inspired Kevin on their first date ...

when he insisted that Sharon paid for dinner ...

Who would have thought that Kevin was such a radical feminist?'

This is a very short and slightly distorted version of what did really happen that night. In fact, they split the cost of the meal, but it is funnier to say that Sharon had to pay for it *all*.

(TURN TO BRIDE)

'Sharon, in case you haven't worked out how financially ... um, er ... *(AS IF TACTFULLY STRUGGLING FOR THE RIGHT WORDS TO DESCRIBE SOMETHING UNPALATABLE)* ... shrewd Kevin is ...

I did hear a rumour that, when Kevin goes on holiday, he takes a five pound note and a pair of underpants ...

and he doesn't change either of them.

Old gag, but again a nice fit to exaggerate the truth.

(PAUSE...SLIGHT CHANGE OF TONE FOR SHORT SERIOUS BIT)

'For many years, for me, Kevin has been a financial adviser, a golf partner, a drinking buddy and someone to share a lot of good times with.

And when times were not so good, he has also been someone who I could phone at 3am if I really needed to.

Psychologists always say that you only make five really close friends in a whole lifetime.

It is my privilege that Kevin is one of mine.

It will soon be time to wave you off on your honeymoon.

By the way Kevin, this is a very generous choice on your part ... a package deal for two weeks in Heathrow Terminal 5.

This was a simple topical reference to the horrors that BA passengers were going through at the time.

'I hope that this is the first of many honeymoons that you have with each other ... and I wish you many years to enjoy them.'

The serious bit

The example above includes a certain number of sentences that are entirely serious. They don't have to be particularly clever, but they do have to be completely sincere. You are almost giving a spoken character reference … but one you are bringing to life by adding emotional content to the bare facts.

It is totally wrong for the best man to then propose another toast, as there is no-one else available to make a reply. The best man rounds everything off. There shouldn't be a dry seat in the house.

Father of the Bride

The father of the bride usually makes the first speech which has to be a fine blend of affection for the daughter, warmth to the groom and welcoming benevolence to the guests. There is less pressure on the father of the bride to be funny than there is on the best man, perhaps because the audience is aware that he may have made a significant contribution to the cost of everyone having such a good time.

The anecdote selection and sharpening process is just as important as it is for the best man. The speech can include a couple of gags about the bride's character quirks, as long as there is no risk of this offending the bride. In the following example, the Father of the Bride took advantage of something that had been a running joke between father and daughter – her communication habits – which he exploited nicely without pushing the comedy envelope too far.

> *'I do hope that Olivia's new husband keeps earning a lot of money. He will eventually be able to afford the operation to have the mobile phone removed from her ear.'*

The father (or his nominee) should finish by proposing a toast to the Bride and Groom.

My own father stunned and delighted the audience at the wedding of my sister, Sue. He was always a generous host, but hated time to be wasted by people who talked too much. This affably Bare Knuckle attitude was reflected in the style and length of his toast to the bride and groom, the entire text of which is transcribed below:

> *'Ladies and Gentlemen, I welcome you all and I want to you to enjoy the wedding of my lovely daughter as much as I am.*
>
> *So ... the bar will be open all night, and I'm paying.*
>
> *My toast is ... the bride and groom.'*

Bridegroom

Grooms usually have a few things on their mind. Effective preparation for making a speech is not usually one of them. However, there is no way that they can escape this one. The only comfort we can give is the fact that he is under the least pressure to be funny. Mind you, if he *is* funny, everyone will be delighted.

The typical groom's speech consists of an unending list of gratefully obsequious platitudes. This is an excellent way of boring the audience.

Obviously, there are several people who should be thanked. But to be really successful, the groom's speech must combine gratitude with brevity *and* entertainment.

He can certainly include at least one pointed anecdote about the best man, in the certain knowledge that this treatment will be comprehensively reciprocated. Both sets of parents should certainly be mentioned affectionately, especially if any of them have helped to pay for the day.

The speech should finish by expressing thanks for the previous toast, and the End Spike should be a toast to the bridesmaids.

Eulogies

Eulogies are right at the emotional end of the presentational spectrum. The desired Finishing Position is nearly always the same: that the audience should remember the deceased in a way that makes them smile and cry in a fond and loving way.

An episode of a TV series shows a scene where someone was in the position of suddenly having to 'say a few words' over the grave of another character who had just been buried:

> *'Tom Smith was a person of great faith and a better man than I will ever be. I am really sorry that I murdered him.'*

Bear in mind this crass insensitivity as something you should avoid at all costs.

Preparation

I recommend that eulogies should last no longer than eight minutes. You will have to write out the words verbatim and then use a full script to work from. The reason for this is that it would be almost impossible for you to use notes on cards and also control your emotions.

During the brainstorming and filtering phase of preparation, try to find a selection of anecdotes that capture the most interesting highlights of the person's life. Resist your natural urge to tell the audience absolutely everything. This is not the time for a detailed biography, but it is most definitely the time to remember the very best things.

Delivery

If you are a family member or a close friend of the deceased, you may well have a lot of other things to do before the funeral service. Nevertheless, you must try to rehearse out loud as much as possible. It may be very painful for you to say some of the words you have written, but it is vital you feel that pain in private before you try to cope with it in public.

Definitely use any lectern that there is in the church as a place to put your written script. You may well remember that I mentioned in a previous chapter that using a written script you should aim to make eye contact with the audience 80% of the time. You will *not* be able to do this when you are doing a eulogy. There will be so many sad but sympathetic faces looking at you, that this level of eye contact may make you lose control of your emotions and your delivery.

I recently attended the funeral of a university friend of mine. His best friend from school delivered the main eulogy. It was a superb blend of anecdotes that captured the real joy involved in knowing the deceased. I could see that the speaker had to make a huge effort just to get through his six minutes behind the lectern and he rarely looked up from his script. He also found it difficult to put much conversational light and shade into his delivery. However, we could all feel the same emotion as him. The sheer intensity of his agony was absolutely clear. We all knew it was a superb achievement for him just to get to the end of the speech and we were profoundly touched.

I learned something from this. I realized that my rigid recommendation to suck-and-spew is just not practical when emotions are highly charged. As long as you have put in sufficient effort in the words of the eulogies, and rehearsed enough to dampen down at least some of your emotions, simply getting through the words in an audible way is enough for you to get the result you want. If eye contact gets in the way of your performance, just don't try it.

Below, I have re-produced an extract of a eulogy given by one of my clients (referred to as 'the speaker') at the funeral of his father, Peter. It was exactly the right combination of sensitivity, seriousness and smiles.

The structure he used was:

Beginning Spike

Key Elements:

1. Childhood

2. Wartime

3. Character Aspects

4. Marriage, Parenthood and Community

5. Spiritual Beliefs

Micro-Statement

End Spike

Here is a lengthy extract, with my comments on what he achieved in each phase of the presentation:

'Dad was successful at many things. But what he really wanted to do was to sail and beachcomb in the South Seas.'

This was a very effective First Spike, grabbing the audience's attention with something that most of them did not know.

'Remember this and you have captured the core of his character.'

After dealing with Peter's childhood, the speaker went on to describe some of his wartime experiences:

'He was then selected to train with the United States Navy as an aviator. He graduated near the top of his class on that savagely tough course made famous by the movie "An Officer and a Gentleman".

Dad flew Dive Bombers. Such pilots had a life expectancy of less than three months and so they were given a lot of freedom when it came to petty rules.

This suited Dad just fine!

Dad's American C.O. wrote a report on Dad in the following terms:

"No sense of religion, no sense of patriotism, no sense of out of flight discipline. But a fine brave aviator. When we attack the Japanese Homes Islands I want him in my squadron."

Dad came away from the war with a clear sense that your fate was in your own hands.

Dad worked hard all his life ....

Although he took early retirement on his 80th birthday.'

A gentle gag which got a big laugh.

'In many ways he was anti-authoritarian.

He did however have a moral compass.

Albeit one that had not been recalibrated since 1945!

He had a clear sense of doing the right thing. Of being steadfast. Of standing up for what he thought was right.

You might call him a modest man.

But he wasn't the sort who would spend any time thinking about his many achievements so that he could decide whether to be modest or not.

He did not look for popularity. But was popular.

He was a social man but not a socializer.

A charming man but not a charmer.

He believed that honour is a gift that a man gives to himself.

It cannot be taken away from you, it can only be given away.

He believed all such things quietly.

He would never dream of imposing them on others.

He also firmly believed it was his duty to contribute to the community.

He was the same person with all people

... provided he liked them, that is.

The sequence of short sentences allowed the speaker to go into some depth about Peter's character, without seeming to dwell too long.

'He met Mum in Southampton at a Royal Marines Ball that he gate-crashed in 1949. That was the start of a love that formed the centre of Dad's life.

A love that lasted over fifty years.

Mum both complimented and softened Dad.

He adored her and she adored him.

Mum was often seriously ill but Dad nursed her and cherished her throughout.

He was often impatient and could, just occasionally, be short tempered especially when he encountered beaurocracy or stupidity.

With Mum he was incredibly gentle and patient.

Supportive whenever she needed him.

He must have found her death devastating when she died some five years ago. He shed the occasional soft quiet tear. He must have been lonely but never complained or sought pity.

Dad was not really a material minded person.

True, he did like his car and he loved his boat.

But he didn't want material possessions.

He had the same watch and pen knife for 40 years.

And the same socks since World War Two.'

A clever exaggeration to round off a serious section with a strong laugh.

'This last year was tough for Dad.

But even as he saw his independence whittled away day by day, he was stoic and dignified.

He managed to find humour in his condition.

Many times these last 12 months we thought it was the end.

Each time he would come back, against the odds.

Indeed, he had more rallies than John McEnroe.'

He even manages to make the audience smile at the concept of impending death.

In the next section, the speaker manages to deal with spiritual concepts as well as capturing an important aspect of Peter's character.

'Dad came to think there may well be alternative dimensions.

You see, he had a recurrent dream of him and Mum on a small boat in the South Seas.

He rather thought that would be a pretty fine dimension to slip into.

On the other hand, he also thought he would like to come back as a family dog.

A life-force as strong and bright as Dad's must go somewhere. Maybe to heaven, maybe to another dimension, maybe even reincarnation.

So the next time you see a scallywag mutt on the prow of a yacht, nose to the South West Wind, ears flapping like flags and sea fever in his eyes. Look hard.

Because you never know!'

The speaker finally encapsulates what his dad meant to him in a very simple Micro-Statement, before delivering an End Spike that everyone who heard it still remembers:

'Peter was my father. He was a great friend of mine, and I will miss him terribly.

Dad believed he was not defined by his interests or profession.

Asked to define himself he would have said simply 'A Manxman'.

That is how he would want us to remember him.'

I am certain that the speaker's words, especially his last ones, would have made his father smile.

At the end of the eulogy for my mother (affectionately known as 'Moth'), I deliberately played the emotion card as hard as possible in my End Spike. I felt it was my duty to end with something that could give the congregation the chance to shed some tears if they needed to. I also wanted to make sure that they truly appreciated the detailed, loving touches that my sister, Sue, brought to my mother's life:

> *'Moth loved travelling on cruise ships. Before her last cruise, Sue spent weeks lovingly creating a small piece of embroidery which she gave to Moth just before she embarked.*
>
> *It just consisted of two words, in French.*
>
> *Those words captured Sue's wishes for moth then, and they are even more appropriate now as she leaves on her final journey.*
>
> *The words were ... BON VOYAGE.'*

Complaining

Many people unfairly assume that I sometimes actually enjoy complaining. The accusation is inaccurate because I *always* enjoy complaining.

This is a situation where you need to be able to control and channel your emotional involvement before deciding on the words you want to say. If you let your anger control your presentation, you are likely to blurt out a Spike like:

> *'I just can't believe how incompetent you people are. We shouldn't have to pay 800 dollars a night to be treated like dirt. Are you doing this deliberately, or are you just stupid?'*

Be honest with yourself here. Even if you have never been daft enough to say those words to the staff of an expensive hotel when you have been on a plane for 11 hours and they can't find your reservation … *you have certainly wanted to.* Sadly, I have not only wanted to, but I have given voice to that desire many times before I realized that my presentation technique needed a little toning down.

Let's apply the Pipeline to the above situation:

Knockout result: The hotel gives us a complimentary suite for a week, with lots of champagne and a great deal of obscene grovelling.

Audience analysis: shows that the staff have a Starting Position of real concern for my situation and they are very keen to do anything reasonable to remedy the situation.

Finishing position: Being reasonable myself, I will settle for a bit of grovelling, a bottle of champagne and a free dinner.

Micro-Statement: You will have to make a lot of effort to sort all this out, but if you do, I will be happy.

Key Elements:

1. What you would expect for the cost.

2. What has actually happened to you.

3. What you would like done about it.

First Spike: *'The last time my girlfriend came to Barbados, it was her 40th birthday and she was on her own. This time I want her to have the nicest birthday of her life, but instead we have had to wait an hour for our room. I hope you can understand why we are so upset.'*

End Spike: *'I hope you can come up with something that means we have really good memories of the service here, rather than sad and angry ones.'*

We got the suite (not free, but the same rate as a standard room), a complimentary dinner, two bottles of champagne and an amount of grovelling that teetered along the borderline between obscene and profane.

Key lessons:

- Control and express your emotion; don't let your emotion control you.
- Be sensitive to whether the audience really wants to help
- Ensure that your desired Finishing Position does not amount to extortion
- Make sure that your First Spike is devastatingly sharp, without being abusive
- Speak in a voice that is slightly quieter than normal
- Look for opportunities to smile instead of scowl.

Getting an Upgrade

Your main weapon in this situation has to be sheer, Bare Knuckle charm. Let's face it, getting thousands of pounds worth of upgrade is a really Knockout Result. The key to success is total focus during even the most casual interaction with airline staff at the airport.

A few years ago, I flew out to the USA on airline X and had a horrible time. The seats were Lilliputian in size and the flight attendants had the customer service skills I would associate with paratroopers. So, when I arrived at the airport for my return journey, I was steeled for another 11 hours of unpleasantness.

However, I was delighted to discover that, because of a code-sharing arrangement, my return flight was going to be on a plane from airline Y. It gave me the chance to exploit the situation and improve my environment for the flight home. I used this Spike right at the start of the conversation with the Y check-in clerk:

'I am so delighted to be flying with you instead of X, that I don't really mind where you seat me, because I know it's going to be a great experience anyway.'

I then told them about my nightmare with X, and contrasted it with my previous Y travels. I managed to slip in a Micro-Statement:

'Other carriers may think they are the world's favourite, but you are certainly mine.'

Reading this in cold print on a page, you may be cringing a bit. You might think that cynical staff have heard all this before, and that I was ladling on the treacle in over-enthusiastic quantities. Nevertheless, just as I was boarding the plane, the guy who had checked me in beckoned me to one side, took my economy class boarding pass and gave me one for Seat 1A in First Class.

I had achieved a Double Knockout Result, because he had missed Premium Economy out of the process and upgraded me by *two* classes.

The key to my success was being able to bring some real emotional content to my delivery of the Spike and Micro-Statement. My carefully worded presentation was also utterly genuine.

More recently, I was checking in another airline counter in Bangkok Airport. I had already been warned by email that the flight was going to be delayed for several hours, so I had not rushed to the airport. There was no queue. A swift Audience Analysis meant that I bore in mind the sort of angry words that the staff must have been hearing from all their customers for the previous two hours. I also took into account that Thai people greatly respect those who can remain smiling and dignified in adversity.

So, beaming with as many teeth as possible, my Spike was:

'I am sure that everyone has been angry with you this evening, but I will be happy if you can get me on some sort of plane some time over the next 12 hours.'

No less than four Thai check-in staff bowed and beamed back at me. The chief clerk actually said, 'You are the first person tonight who has spoken to us with a smile'.

Her subordinate had already decided to upgrade me from Economy to World Traveller Plus, but after some conferring and smiley nods, I was again handed the Holy Grail: a two thousand-pound flat-bed-and-loads-of-champagne business class seat.

As I left the check-in area, my audience had grown to seven people who I still feel wanted to burst into a round of applause. I like to think that if I had carried on talking to them, I could have ended up next to the Pilot.

But enough of my fantasies. Here are the crucial ingredients for Bare Knuckle Upgrade-grabbing:

- Don't check-in online. Make sure that you can interact with a human being.
- See if there is anything in the situation that day that you can take advantage of.
- Use a Spike and a Micro-Statement that sound and *feel* genuine.

I very much hope that one day we will meet one day in a business class departure lounge on an occasion where the comfort of our travel has been assured by the effectiveness of the Bare Knuckle method rather than the size of our wallets.

Pipeline Summary

KNOCKOUT
Decide what the best conceivable result would be

ANALYSIS
Ask Who, Why, Want, Need, Must.

POSITIONS
Establish their Starting Position and your desired Finishing Position

STATEMENT
Create an encapsulating Micro-Statement

BRAINSTORM
Generate headings from the Micro-Statement

FILTERS
Drive the headings through the Factual Filter and the Anti-Filter

ELEMENTS
Turn the headings into an ordered list of Key Elements

WRITE
Write out the words that support each heading

EDIT
Edit the words down to create Baseline Text

SPIKE
Add a First Spike and an End Spike

NAIL
Transfer your content to cards, paper or auto-cue

KEY BARE KNUCKLE TERMINOLOGY

A **Knockout Result** is what, in an utterly ideal world, you would like to accomplish with your target audience.

The **Starting Position** is what the audience thinks, knows or feels about your presentational topic before you start your presentation.

The **Finishing Position** is what you want the audience to think, know or feel at the *end* of the presentation, having taken into account the full practical reality of the situation.

A **Micro-Statement** is a sequence of words that quickly and compellingly captures the essence of your presentation *in a way that is specifically shaped for the needs of a specific audience at a particular time.*

The **Key Elements** are the headings which make up the core of the main body of a presentation.

The **Baseline Text** is a version of the presentation which contains about 70% of the words tat you will actually say on the day.

A **Spike** is a sequence of words that is sharp and striking enough to grab and keep the attention of the audience.

The **First Spike** should make up the first few sentences of your presentation.

The **End Spike** should be the last few sentences.

Graham is a recovering barrister and ex-President of the Cambridge Union who has become one of the UK's busiest professional speakers and is certainly its most challenging presentation coach. He has worked as a speaker or coach for just under half the FTSE 100, and his individual clients include Chief Executives, Celebrities, Olympic athletes and 7 members of the Conservative Front Bench. In his role as a Presentation Attack Dog, he is a regular guest on the BBC, Sky News and CNN, analyzing (OK ripping apart) high-profile political speeches.

www.grahamdavies.co.uk

www.straighttalking.co.uk

For enquiries about presentation coaching or speaking engagements, contact Graham via graham@grahamdavies.co.uk or 0207 937 7758.

ACKNOWLEDGEMENTS

My friends in the Professional Speaking Association have inspired, entertained, and supported me unequivocally. The following were vital to my sanity while I was writing: Paul Bridle, Warren Evans, Lesley Everett, Tim Gard, Jane Gunn, Roger Harrop, Graham Jones, Paul McGee, Roy Sheppard and Alan Stevens.

Dan Bond has been my business partner, coach, patient friend and the originator of a huge number of the concepts in this book. Dan, thank you for always being there.

Kate Oldfield has been a superb midwife for my first written baby. I recommend her to anyone writing a book, especially their first.

The caring IT expertise of Hunain Dosani and Tracey Kane has been invaluable, as was the advice of Allan Sams, Chris Steele and Steve Shay.

Thank you to Andrew Corlett for being my tireless *consiglier* and to David Calderhead for being someone I could phone at 3am.

Thank you to Gideon Joseph, for his energy, loyalty and faith.

Thank you to Marek Kriwald for being daft enough to make a cold call to Capstone.

Finally, thank you to Nicole Gates for always believing in this book, for agreeing to go on our first date 25 years after we met, and for only making me wait 4 years for the second one.

INDEX

80/20 Rule, 109

After-Dinner, 152, 180, 194
Agenda, 46–47, 119, 165, 235, 237
Andrew Corlett, 200
Anecdote Selection, 246–247, 250
Answering Questions, 163–165, 227–228
Anti Filter, 54, 58–61, 263
Anxiety, 1, 9, 139
Attention Spans, 199
Audience Analysis, 5–6, 19
Audience Focus, 13, 16, 25, 128
Audience Layout, 152
Audience Research, 30
Audience Zones, 244–245
Audio-visual Anaesthesia, 118
Autocue, 100
Award Ceremonies, 100

Backgrounds, 127
Bar Stool, 231
Barack Obama, 43, 112
Baseline Text, 71–72, 81, 97, 101–102, 119, 137
Battle Conditions, 138, 151

Best Man's Speech, 244
Best-Man Syndrome, 246
Blending, 179, 188–190
Boardrooms, 8, 13, 153, 162
Body Language, 147–148
Brainstorm, 5, 15, 33, 51–55, 58, 61, 65, 67, 226
Builds, 125, 127–129
Bullet Points, 113, 120–124, 214

Cards, 105–107
Cartoons, 187
Centipede, 55, 58, 64
Churchill, 34, 62, 92, 147
Clanger, 63–64
Clarifying Positions, 28–30
Comedy Writers, 186
Comfort Zone, 84
Comfy Sofa, 231
Common Denominators, 16, 28
Complaints, 12, 47, 243, 256, 258–260
Conference Organizers, 212–214
Confidence, 105, 155, 180, 191, 236

Conversational Tone, 141–142
Crown Court, 91

David Cameron, 12, 46,
    98–100
David Davis, 98
Default Slides, 126
Derek Hatton, 107
Dialogue, 142, 169
Diction, 144
Differentiation, 46–47
Dinner Party Intensity, 143,
    155, 224

Editing, 6–7, 9, 72, 101–102,
    108, 136, 240
Emotions, 252–253
Environment, 9, 13, 73, 138,
    151–154
Eulogies, 251–252
Executive Summaries, 123–124
Eye Contact, 144–145

Factual Filter, 54–58, 60–61, 65
Factual Foundation, 246
Father of the Bride Speech,
    250–251
Filters, 54, 58–61
Finishing Position, 22, 29,
    30–31, 36–38, 42, 46–47,
    178, 195, 200, 251, 259–260,
    263, 265
FIR Formula, 170–172
First Spike, 78–79, 84, 93–95,
    221, 238–239, 254, 259–260
Floor Monitors, 113
Formal Presentations, 228

Gestures, 143, 148, 150, 161
Grouping, 61–62

Hamlet, 76–78
Hand-held Microphones, 156

Handouts, 214–215
Hecklers, 107
Hostility, 168
House Keeping, 87, 89, 118,
    163, 216, 237
Humour Selection, 178, 187,
    190

Iain Duncan Smith, 42, 90
Impersonations, 187
Infatuations, 188
Inside Jokes, 178
Insta-Absorb, 122, 129, 132
Insult Gags, 184, 202
Interaction, 25, 88, 125, 163,
    229, 237, 260

James Bond, 77–78, 231
John Dolan, 204
John F Kennedy, 100, 115
Joke Websites, 185–186

Key Elements, 64–65, 119, 123,
    179, 197–199, 220, 230, 234,
    237, 239, 244, 253, 259
Knock out Result, 15, 18–20,
    22, 30–31, 33, 200, 219,
    259–260

Lapel Microphones, 156, 158
Laptops, 71
Last-minute Requests, 238–240
Lazer Pointers, 159–160
Lectern Microphones, 155
Lecterns, 157–160
Lighting, 154, 157

Macro Statements, 35, 38
Media Interviews, 12, 228,
    234–235
Mehrabian, 147–148
Memory, 98–100, 102, 115,
    123, 179, 207, 228

Microphones, 106, 155
Micro-Statement, 4, 6, 36–42,
    45–52, 54–55, 60, 64–65,
    70, 74, 78, 254, 257, 259,
    261–262, 265

Nerves, 9, 135, 137, 139–140,
    160
Nick Clegg, 1
Notes, 101–104

One-Liners, 181, 247
On-stage Interviews, 228–231
Oscar Wilde, 178

Pace, 102, 146–147, 162
Panel Discussion, 12, 228,
    232–234
Paper Scripts, 8, 108–110
Patronising, 75
Pause & Spike, 173–175
Plasma Screens, 112–113
Pleasantries, 7, 48, 86, 90, 200,
    204, 208, 236
Power Point, 8
Power Point Pipeline, 125–129
Practice, 138–139
Preparation Pipeline, 2, 4, 7, 21,
    26–27
Presentational Myth, 116–117
Professional Speaking
    Association, 100
Public Events, 156, 214

Q & A Strategy, 165
Questions for Audience, 23,
    25, 86
Quotations, 184–186

Racism, 187–188
Reality Check, 212
Re-Channelling, 139, 169
Rubbernecking, 113

Seating Blocks, 153
Self-Deprecation, 90, 201
Sexism, 187
Sexual History, 246
Sit-down Presentations, 223
Slide Commandments, 120,
    124
Slide Mindset, 119
Slides, 214–215
Smile, 177–184
Speaking Slot, 211–212
Spikes, 86, 90, 94, 119–120,
    234, 237
SSS Formula, 172–175
Stage Management, 151–152
Stand Microphones, 9, 106,
    144, 152, 155, 208, 246
Starting Position, 22,
    28–30, 36
Stories, 10, 47, 207, 243, 245
Structure, 74–81
Suck and Spew, 109, 158, 253
Summary, 60–63

Team Leader, 226–227
Team Pitches, 12
Team Presentations, 225–227
Telephone Conferences, 13,
    235–238
Terrors, 58–60, 65
Theft, 91, 131, 186
Time Limits, 44–48
Topical Gags, 182, 185
Triumphs, 10, 58, 60, 65
Tummy Clench, 139–140

Upgrades, 243, 260–262

Voice Control, 141

Walk-up Music, 157, 216
Writing Out, 29, 68–71,
    230